HEPPLEWHITE
SHERATON
&
REGENCY
FURNITURE

SHERATON CARVED, INLAID AND DECORATED SATINWOOD CABINET. Presented by Admiral Viscount Horatio Nelson to Lady Hamilton in Naples *circa* 1800. *Vide* p 45. The handles of a most distinctive Dublin ormolu pattern never appearing on any London productions; thus they, too, are of real significance to all serious students of Georgian furniture designs . . . *Vide* also Pl 178 and 191. Courtesy of the National Gallery of Victoria, Melbourne.

HEPPLEWHITE SHERATON & REGENCY

FURNITURE

BY

F. LEWIS HINCKLEY

379 ILLUSTRATIONS

THE TAURIS
ANTIQUES PRESS
London

Published in 1990 by
The Tauris Antiques Press
110 Gloucester Avenue
London NW1 8JA

British Library Cataloguing in Publication Data
Hinckley, F. Lewis
    Hepplewhite, Sheraton and Regency furniture.
    1. English Furniture, history
    I. Title
    749.22

    ISBN 1-85043-254-6

Manufactured in the United States of America.

TO RALPH G. MARTIN

Contents

A Demographic Statement and LONDON versus so-called OLD ENGLISH Furniture

AFTER THE FIRST of my *Directorys* had remained in print for over twenty-five years, I was requested by one of its later purchasers to justify my demographic statement. This was obviously in reference to its verification of the relative sizes and hence the comparative commercial importance of Europe's largest cities during the eighteenth and early nineteenth centuries. That inquiry did not indicate any interest on the part of a furniture collector, lay writer, or museum official concerned with the study and/or appreciation of so-called *Old English Furniture*. It was made by a publisher who in a matter of minutes might easily have obtained a confirmation of my demographic statement by simply consulting the pertinent records of populations in the Fifth Avenue Branch of the New York Public Library.

Those records show that after only Paris and London, Dublin was formerly the third largest metropolis in Greater Europe, and thus in the entirety of the western world. Nonetheless, ever since the turn of the nineteenth century it has been generally ignored by those to whom such information should have been fundamental to their adopted fields of expertise; Dublin, like every other important capital city, must formerly have produced and distributed its own supplies of distinctively designed and finely executed furniture and looking glasses. As a result of those oversights Dublin's choice, highly valuable, often richly fanciful, and especially decorative productions in both fields, have been habitually misinterpreted as "English"; as attributable to such famous London masters as Thomas Chippendale, Thomas Johnson, William Vile, etc.; with the recent appearances of certain especially extravagant Dublin rarities in the London antique market, they have been attributed to John Channon, Pierre Langlois, or other craftsmen whose London addresses have been recorded, but whose actual work is quite unknown.

Leading writers on the subject have agreed that *English furniture was made principally for royalty and the nobility* and as a result *very little is extant.* Although their researches may not have extended so far back, their opinions are fully substantiated in the collectors' magazines that were published during the turn of the nineteenth century. In these the advertisements of London antique dealers offer their importations of Dutch, Italian, French, and other Continental furniture, but little or nothing that can be recognized as English. Occasional examples of Irish-Chippendale pieces attest to the fact that a few owners of old Irish residences were then parting with the least attractive of their furnishings.

Through the undeniable evidence of those early photographic illustrations it is also obvious why members of the British aristocracy, aware that high-quality Queen Anne and Georgian furniture was absent in the London antique market, had already turned to Dublin for their furnishing or refurbishing needs. Thus in acquiring a Chippendale ribband-back settee and six chairs for Nostel Priory in about 1883,[1] Lord St. Oswald must have obtained these in Dublin, rather than London. Also, we now know that Lady Randolph Churchill during her Ireland years (1877-1881) was able to obtain choice pieces from ancestral homes in her rounds of the Dublin antique shops.[2]

The continued absence of fine Queen Anne and Georgian furniture in London during the later decades of the nineteenth century kept American antique dealers and interior decorators away from that market until about 1903. It was in that year that Daniel Farr found he could obtain the same high-quality (Dublin) merchandise in London under more comfortable circumstances. As owner of a most successful New York City antique shop, he (and his wealthy clientele) could well afford the one extra profit exacted by this easy change in his itinerary.

When English antique dealers joined those from the United States in patronizing the Dublin market and sometimes in also dealing directly with owners of old Irish residences, the same magazine advertisements show a gradually increasing panorama of distinctive Dublin seat furniture, cabinetwork, and looking glasses. Also, from 1905 on there was a steady increase of publications in book form dealing with the subject of so-called Old English Furniture. These were routinely illustrated with the earliest Dublin imports to have arrived in England, some even prior to the 1900s, and then with many others as they continued arriving throughout the succeeding decades of the present century.

All such masterpieces received in London and New York during the last hundred years have been capital city productions of which there are no London counterparts. Nevertheless, all have been arbitrarily accepted by museum and literary authorities as *English*—that is, as having been designed and executed in some nonexistent metropolitan furniture center of the Midlands, the North Country, or some other English provincial area outside of London.

In contrast, every bona fide London production has always been recognized and acknowledged as such in all leading British and American museums and publications. In that regard it will be noticed that even to this day *LONDON* labels are extremely scarce in museum exhibits of Queen Anne and Georgian furniture and looking glasses, especially in comparison with those of the more numerous unrecognized Dublin masterpieces that are, and always have been, mistakenly labeled as *ENGLISH*.

That relatively small number of genuine London examples, in comparison with those of the more productive sister capital, also agrees with the observations of Parisian authorities who have drawn attention to the very few known former London cabinetmakers and joiners vis-à-vis the far greater number of known Parisian *ébénistes* and *menuisiers* who were registered in their officially regulated city guilds. Those particular differences will remain constant despite any possible further attempt to increase the number of *The London Furniture Makers*[3] through publishing the names and street addresses of unknown woodworkers indiscriminately gleaned from their listings in old *London Directorys*.

As to documentary evidence, pedigrees such as those accompanying the relatively few important London productions that have been permitted to reach the public market have but seldom accompanied the innumerable transfers of ancestral pieces that have been removed from old Irish castles and mansions throughout the last hundred years. Such omissions are attributable mainly to the fact that generations of American and English traders, in keeping with sound business practice, have refrained from voluntarily disclosing their private and/or commercial sources of supply.

1. Edwards and Jourdain, *Georgian Cabinet-Makers,* London, 1955, p. 70.
2. Ralph G. Martin, *Jennie,* Vol. 1, London, 1969.
3. Sir Ambrose Heal, *The London Furniture Makers, 1660-1840,* London, 1953.

Collections: A Partial Listing

IMPORTANT ORIGINAL COLLECTIONS, inheritors, and acquirers of fine Dublin furniture based upon mistakenly labeled examples illustrated in the literature on *Old English* and *Early American Furniture*.

Addington, Lord
Alexandra, H. R. H. Queen
ALTHROP, NORTHAMPTONSHIRE (SPENCER FAMILY)
Amherst Collection
Arkwright, Sir Richard
Armagh, Bishop of
Ashburnham Place, *Sussex*
Asheton-Smith, Lady
Ashintully Castle, *Perthshire*
Avebury Manor, *Wiltshire*
BADMINTON HOUSE, GLOUCESTERSHIRE (DUKE OF BEAUFORT)
Balfour, Earl *East Lothian, Scotland*
BEAUFORT, DUKE OF, BADMINTON HOUSE, GLOUCESTERSHIRE
BEIT, SIR ALFRED, ROSSBOROUGH HOUSE
Belgard Castle
Benjamin, E. H.
Benkard, Mrs. Henry Horton
Berleigh Abbey, *Essex*
Bernal Collection
Bessborough, Earl of Ingres Abbey
Bevan Collection, *Littlecote*
Biecester of Tusmore, Lord
Bigelow Collection
Bigelow, Francis H.
Blackwell, Geoffrey
Blackwell, John
BLAISE CASTLE, BRISTOL
Blenheim Castle (Duke of Marlborough)
Bodelwyddan Castle, *North Wales*
BOOTHBAY FAMILY, GORHAM, MAINE
BORDELEY, DR. JAMES, JR.
Bourne Park, *Canterbury*
Bower House, *Havering-Atte-Bower*
BOWES, SIR WILLIAM, STREATLAN CASTLE

BOYCE COURT, GLOUCESTERSHIRE
Boyton House, *Wiltshire*
Brady, Genevieve Garvan, *New York*
BRAMSHILL, HAMPSHIRE
Bringhurst, Edward, *Wilmington, Delaware*
Brockenhurst Park
Brockie, James A.
Brooks family, *Cambridge, Massachusetts*
Browett, E. M.
Brown, F. D.
BRUCE, MRS. J.
BRYMPTON D'ENERCY, SOMERSET (SIR SPENCER PONSONBY FANE)
BUCCLEUCH, DUKE OF MONTAGUE HOUSE
Buck, John H., *Hartford, Connecticut*
Buckingham, Duke of
BUCKINGHAM PALACE, Royal Apartments
Bull, C. Sanford, *Watertown, Connecticut*
Burdett, Sir Francis
Burghley House
Burton, Frank E.
Buxted Park, *Sussex* (Lord Portman)
Cabot family, *Boston, Massachusetts*
Caledon, Earl of
Callaly Castle
Carey, Helen H.
CARLTON HOUSE
Carnovan, Earl of Highclere Castle
Carrington family
Carruthers, Col. Wm. F., *Dumfrieshire*
Carter, James Walter
Cary, Castle, *Guernsey, Channel Islands*
CASSIOBURY PARK (EARL OF ESSEX) *Watford, Hertfordshire*
Chandos, Duke of
Chantrey, The Elstree, *Hertfordshire*
Charbonnier, T.

Charlemont, Earl of Charlemont House, *Dublin*
Charlotte, H. R. H. Princess
Charlotte, H. R. H. Queen
Charrington, Guy N.
Charteris, Lady
CHATSWORTH (DUKE OF DEVONSHIRE)
Chelwood Vetchery, *Sussex*
Chesterfield, Earl of Holme Lacy
Chetham's Hospital, *Manchester*
Chevening House
CHOLMONDELEY, MARQUIS OF HOUGHTON
    HALL, *NORFOLK*
Churchill, Lady Randolph
Clarence, Duke of
Clarke, Thomas B.
Cluny, Musée
COBHAM, VISCOUNT HAGLEY HALL,
    WORCESTERSHIRE
Cockerell, Pepys
Colonial Williamsburg
Colville, Captain N. R.
Compton Castle, *Somerset*
Congreve, Mrs. Ambrose
Connaught, Duke of
Connock family, *Trewergey, Cornwall*
Cooke, Helen T., *Wellesley, Massachusetts*
Cooley, Charles P., *Hartford, Connecticut*
COOMBE ABBEY, WARWICKSHIRE
Cooper, James Fenimore, *Cooperstown, New York*
COPPED HALL, ESSEX (LORD DeLISLE AND
    DUDLEY)
Corey, Alan, Jr.
Corsham, Count Wiltshire (Field Marshal Lord
    Methuen)
Cory, S. Campbell
Coventry, Earl of Croome Court
Cradock, Thomas, family
Craven, Baron, Coombe Abbey, *Warwickshire*
Cornelia, Countess of
CRICHEL, DORSET
Crimm, Dr. William H., *Baltimore, Maryland*
Croome Court (Earl of Coventry)
Cross, Major Shepherd
Crowninschild family, *Salem, Massachusetts*
Culzean Castle, Ayrshire
Cumberland, Duke of
Cure, Lady Capel
Cuthbertson, F. H.

Davis, Alfred
Dean, H. Percy, Bridgefoot House, *Buckinghampshire*
Dearborn, General Henry, family, *Maine*
Delapre Abbey
DeLISLE AND DUDLEY, LORD, COPPED HALL,
    ESSEX; *PENHURST PLACE, KENT*
DENSTON HALL, SUFFOLK
Derby, Earl of Knowsley Hall
DeRothschild, Sir Anthony

DEVON, EARL OF *(POWDERHAM CASTLE*, nr
    EXETER, DEVONSHIRE)
DEVONSHIRE, DUKE OF
Dickinson, Capt. W. F.
DICKSON, R. EDEN
Dingley Hall
Dixon, F.
Donaldson Collection
Donaldson, Sir George
Doverdale, Lord
Downe, Viscount, *Wyheham Abbey, Yorkshire*
Drake, Clifford S., *North Hampton*
DRYHAM PARK, GLOUCESTERSHIRE
Dudley House, *London*
DUDLEY NORTH FAMILY
Dumfries House, *Ayrshire*
Dunne, F. L., *Boston, Massachusetts*
DuPont Collection
Dutton, Ralph, Hinton Ampner House
Dysart, Earl of

East, Sir Clayton
Easton Neston
Eden Castle, *Durham*
Edinburgh, Duchess of
Elizabeth, H. R. H. Princess; Duchess of Edinburgh
Ely, Earl of
ENFIELD, VISCOUNT
Erthig Park, *Denbighshire*
ESSEX, EARL OF, CASSIOBURY PARK, *Watford,*
    NW of London
Exeter, Marquis of

Fagge, Sir John
Fairbank, Sir Thomas
FANE, SIR SPENCER PONSONBY, BRYMPTON
    D'ENERCY, SOMERSET
Farley, Major
Fawley Court, *Henly-on-Thames*
Fay, S. Prescott
Fayerweather, John, *Cambridge, Massachusetts*
Fayerweather, Thomas, *Cambridge, Massachusetts*
Fellowes, Mrs. Reginald
Fergusson, Sir James
Fischer, S. T.
Fleishmann, L.
Flitwick Manor, *Bedfordshire*
Foster, John Arnold
Foster, Misses A. and E. P.
Freeland, A. R. Stilwell

Gardiner, Sir Robert
Gardiner, Samuel Harrison
Garvan, Francis P.
GEORGE II, H. R. H. KING
GEORGE III, H. R. H. KING
GEORGE IV, H. R. H. KING
George, W. E.
Getty, J. Paul
Gibbs, H. Martin

GIBBS, MRS, JOHN S., JR.
Gilbey, Sir Walter
Gloucester, Duke of
GOBIET, ARMAND, *BERLIN, GERMANY*
Goldschmidt, Lt.-Col. S. G.
Goodwin, William B.
Goodwood, *Sussex*
Gort, Lord, *Dublin*
Gossage Hall, *Cheshire*
Grace, Mrs. W. R.
Gray family, *Boston, Massachusetts*
Green, Frank
Greville, Sir Sydney
GRIFFITHS, PERCIVAL
Grossmith, Weedon
HAGLEY HALL, WORCESTERSHIRE
    (VISCOUNT COBHAM)
HAGUE, SIR HARRY AND LADY
Halsey, T. Haines, *New York City*
Ham House
Hamilton, Duke of, *Hamilton Palace, Lanarkshire*
HAMILTON, LADY, *NAPLES*
Hammond family, *St. Albans Place, East Kent*
Hammond, William
Hammond-Harwood House
Hancock, John
Hannen, Henry
Hardwick Hall
HAREWOOD HOUSE
Harling Hall, *Norfolk*
Harmsworth, Sir R. L.
Harrington, Earl of, *Elvaston Castle, Derbyshire*
Hart, Mr. and Mrs. Geoffrey
Hartwell House
Harwood family
Haslan, D.
Haslan, G. D.
Hastings, Lord, *Melton Constable*
HATFIELD HOUSE, SURREY, MARQUIS OF
    SALISBURY
Hatzfeldt, Princess, *Foliejon Park*
Hearst, William Randolph
Heathcote family
Heathcote, Col. G. R.
Heaton, Percy
Hereford, Viscount
Heywood-Lonsdale, Lt.-Col. A.
Hibbert, A. Holland
Highclere Castle, *Hampshire* (Earl of Carnovan)
Hill Hall, Essex
Hillingdon, Lord
Hilton, Captain R. S.
Hinton Ampner House (Ralph Dutton)
Hirsch, Henry
Hirsch, Leopold
Holme Lacy, *Herefordshire*
Horlick, Sir James, *London*

HORNBY CASTLE, YORKSHIRE (DUKE OF
    LEEDS)
Horton Lodge, *Epson*
HOUGHTON HALL, NORFOLK (MARQUIS
    OF CHOLMONDELEY)
Howe, Earl
Hudson, Mr. and Mrs. Edward
HUMPHREYS, SIR WILLIAM
HUNGERFORD FAMILY
Hylton, Lord
Hyndford, Earl of
Ickworth
India House
Ingres Abbey, *Kent* (Earl of Bessborough)
Inland Revenue Authorities (Classification as "An
    Article of National Interest")
Ivory, James
Iwerne Minster House, *Dorset*
James, W.
Jenner, Lt.-Col. C. D., *Bath*
Joel, J. J.
Joel, S.
Jones Collection
Karolik Collection
Kedleston (Viscount Scarsdale)
Kempe, C. E.
Kent, Duke and Duchess of
Key, Francis Scott
Keyes, Mrs. Homer Eaton
Kimbolton Castle (Duke of Manchester)
Kindermann, C. H. F.
Kington Maurward, *Dorchester* (Pitt family)
Kinnaird Castle (Earl of Southesk)
Kipper, Katrina
Knight, Mr. and Mrs. Leonard
Langford Court, *Langford, Somerset*
Lansdowne, Earl of
Lansdowne, Marchioness of
Lawrence, Ernest
Leconfield, Lord, *Petworth*
Leeds, Duke of, *Hornby Castle, Yorkshire*
Lees, Sir William Clare
LEIGH, LORD, *STONLEIGH ABBEY*
Leinster, Duke of
Leitrim, Earl of
Letts, Sidney
Leven and Melville, Earl of
Lever, J. H.
Lever, Lady
LEVERHULME, VISCOUNT
Liddell, Robert, *Netherton Hall, Northumberland*
LIMERICK, DOWAGER COUNTESS OF
LINDSAY, SIR GEORGE, *HALFORD,
    GLOUCESTERSHIRE*
Littlecote, *Berkshire*
Littleton, Alfred

Lloyd, Governor Edward, *of Maryland*
Lockwood, Luke Vincent
Lofthouse, S. H. S.
LONDON COMPANIES: THE WORSHIPFUL
　COMPANY OF STATIONERS, MERCERS, ETC.
LONGFORD CASTLE, WILTSHIRE (EARL OF
　RADNOR)
LONSDALE, LORD, *LOWTHER CASTLE*
LOWTHER CASTLE (LORD LONSDALE)
Lulworth Castle
Luton Hoo
Lyons, Lt.-Col. A. B. Croft

Mackinnon, Alan
Macquoid, Percy
Macquoid, Mrs. Percy
Maginn, J. F. H.
Manchester, Duke of, *Kinbolton Castle,*
　Huntingdonshire
MANSFIELD, EARL OF, SCONE PALACE,
　PERTHSHIRE
Mansion House, London
Marlborough House
Marlborough, Duke of, *Blenheim Castle*
MARY, H. R. H. QUEEN
May, Stanley J.
McCann, Charles F.
Meagher, J. J.
Melbourne Hall, *Derbyshire*
Melton Constable (Lord Hastings)
Meredith, W. A.
Methuen, Field Marshal Lord, *Corsham, Wiltshire*
Micklem, General
MILLER, EDGAR G., JR.
Milton Abbey
Mitchell, Sir Herbert
Money, Mrs. M. L. C.
Monksbridge, *Sunbury-on-Thames*
Monson, Lord
MONTAGUE HOUSE (DUKE OF BUCCLEUCH)
Montgomery, Sir Basil
Moray, Earl of, *Kinfauns Castle, Perthshire*
Morgan, J. Pierpont
MORSON, CHARLES R., *NEW YORK CITY*
Mount Vernon Ladies' Association
Mulliner, H. H.
Murray Collection
Myers, Louis G., *New York City*

National Interest, Article of
Neate, Stephen
NELSON, LORD
Nettlecombe, Somerset (Sir Walter Trevelyan)
Nettlecombe Court, Somerset (Mrs. J. A. Wolseley)
Neville, Lady
NEWTON PARK, BRISTOL (EARL TEMPLE)
Normanton Park

NORTH, LADY CHARLOTTE MARIA
NORTH, LORD DUDLEY
NOSTEL PRIORY (LORD ST. OSWALD)
Nugent, Sir Edward Charles
Nutting, Wallace, *Framingham, Massachusetts*

Oakley Hall
Oakley-Livingston family, *New York*
Oatway, T.
Ogston Hall, *Derbyshire*
Old Manor, Olney, *Buckinghamshire*
Onslow, Earl of
Oppenheim, Henry
Orrock, James
Ovington House

Padworth
Palmer, George S.
Parkman, Deacon William
Patterson, R. W. Weir
Paul, J. Gilman D'Arcy
Pelham, J. Thursby
Pembroke, Earl of, *Wilton House*
Pendleton Collection
PENSHURST PLACE, KENT (LORD DeLISLE
　AND DUDLEY)
Perry, Marsden
Petworth House, *Sussex*
Pewsey, Wiltshire
Phillips, Sir Claude
Pierce-Nichols family, *Salem, Massachusetts*
Pinwell, Captain, *Cornwall*
Pitt family, Kinston Maurward, *Dorchester*
Plender, Lord William
Poke, Frederick
PORTLAND, DUKE OF, WELBECK WOOD-
　HOUSE WORKSOP, *NOTTINGHAMSHIRE*
Portman, Lord, *Buxted Park, Sussex*
POWDERHAM CASTLE, nr *Exeter, Devonshire*
Powell family, *Nant-Eos, Cardiganshire*
Prestige, Sir John
PRESTON, MRS. WILLIAM, RICHMOND,
　VIRGINIA
PRIOR PARK BATH
Prothero, Sir George

RADNOR, EARL OF, LONGFORD CASTLE,
　WILTSHIRE
Ragley Hall, *Warwickshire*
Ramsden, Sir John
Ravensworth, Lord, *Ravensworth Castle*
Reed, Brooks
Reed, Frederick Howard
Reed, J. Howard
Reid, Andrew J.
Reifsnyder, Howard, *Philadelphia*
Ribblesdale, Lord, *London*
Rice, E. L.
Richmond, L., *Freehold, New Jersey*

Ripon, Marquis of, *Studleigh*
Robinson, Vincent J.
Rockefeller, Mr. and Mrs. David
Roehampton House
Rokeby Park, *Yorkshire*
Rossborough House (Sir Alfred Beit)
Rossetti, Dante Gabriel
ROTCH, C. D.
Rotch family, *Boston, Massachusetts*
Rothbarth Collection
Rothermere, Lord
Rothschild, Anthony
Roxburgh, Duchess of
Rufford Abbey (Lord Savile)
ST. GILES HOUSE, DORSET (EARL OF
    SHAFTESBURY)
ST. OSWALD, LORD NOSTEL PRIORY
SALISBURY, MARQUIS OF, *HATFIELD HOUSE,*
    SURREY
Saltram
Sanderson, Edward F.
Sassoon, Sir. P.
Savile, Lord, *Rufford Abbey*
Scarsdale, Viscount, *Kedleston*
Schreiber, Lady Charlotte
Schuyler, General Philip John
SCONE PALACE, PERTHSHIRE (Earl of
    Mansfield)
Scott, Dr. Lindley
SHAFTESBURY, EARL OF, *ST. GILES HOUSE,*
    DORSET
Shire End, *Perthshire*
Shobden Court, *Hertfordshire*
Sidney, H. M., *Surtees House*
Sill, Mrs. Howard
Smith, Lady Asheton
Smith, Robert T., *Hartford, Connecticut*
Smithills Hall, *Lancashire*
Snyder, Mrs. C. Edward
Southest, Earl of, *Kinnaird Castle*
SPENCER FAMILY, ALTHORP,
    NORTHAMPTONSHIRE
Star and Garter Hotel, *Kew Bridge*
Steinberg, Jack
Stephens, Rev. J. O.
STONLEIGH ABBEY (LORD LEIGH)
STOURHEAD
Strafford, Cora, Countess of
Strangsteel, Sir Samuel
STREATLAN CASTLE (SIR WILLIAM BOWES)
Sykes, J. S.
SYON HOUSE

Taney, Chief Justice Roger Brooke, *Baltimore,*
    Maryland
Tankerville, Earl of, *Chillingham Castle*
Taylor, J. H., *Newstead, Birstall, Leicestershire*

TEMPLE, EARL, *NEWTON PARK, BRISTOL*
Thursby-Pelham, James
Tipping, Colonel Fearon
TOLLAND, JOHN C.
TOWERS, MRS. ALBERT G.
Trent Park, *Hertfordshire*
Trevelyan, Sir Walter John, *Nettlecombe, Somerset*
Trewergey Manor, *Cornwall* (Connock family)
Trinity Hospital, *Greenwich*
TURNBULL, BAYARD
Tutway, Charles
Tyndall, Miss.
Tyson-Roebling family, *Philadelphia*
Tyttenhanger, *Hertfordshire*

Untermeyer, Irwin
Uppark, Petersfield
Upton House, *Warwickshire*

VanAllen, Mrs. John E.
Van Duersen family, *New York City*
Van Ness, Carroll
van Rennsselaer, Mrs. Killiam K.
Vavasseur, Admiral
Vivian, Capt. Hugh

Wadsworth family, *Salem, Massachusetts*
Wakehurst Place
Walpole, Sir Robert
Wardour Castle, *Wiltshire*
Warwick, Earl of, *Warwick Castle, Warwick*
WASHINGTON, MARTHA
Weeks, Harry W., *Framingham, Massachusetts*
WEIL, HENRY V., *NEW YORK CITY*
WELBECK WOODHOUSE (DUKE OF
    PORTLAND) WORKSOP,
    NOTTINGHAMSHIRE
Wellington, Duke and Duchess of
Welsh University, *Aberystwyth*
Wentworth, Governor John, *New Hampshire*
Wentworth Woodhouse
Wernher, Col. Sir Harold and Lady Zia
West, Jordan, family, *Worcester, Massachusetts*
Westover Mansion, *Virginia*
Westwood Park, *Droitwich*
WHITE, MRS. MILES, JR.
Wilkinson, Sir Russel
Willett, H.
William IV, H. R. H. King
Williams, Stanley, *Hartford, Connecticut*
Williamsburg, Colonial
Wilson, Lady Isabella D.
Wilton, Earl of
Wilton House (Earl of Pembroke)
Winterthur
Winthrop family, *New York, N.Y.*
WINTHROP, E. B. T., *NEW YORK, N.Y.*
Wolseley, Lady

Wolseley Hall, *Staffordshire*
Worsborough Hall, *Barnsley*
WORSHIPFUL COMPANY OF STATIONERS,
    MERCERS, ETC.

Wright family
Wythes, E. J.
YALE, ELIHU
Zurlo, Prince

Acknowledgements

ACCORDING TO ALL British lay authorities on Old English Furniture, and in particular every lay expert on Irish furniture, every one of the masterpieces illustrated in this volume was designed and executed *in England*. Thus they have assumed that during the Queen Anne and Georgian years Ireland was unable to produce any furniture other than that which, throughout the past seventy-five years, they have illustrated and described as provincial in character. A first attempt toward drawing attention to the fact that this was decidedly untrue, and that Ireland, like every other country of commercial and social importance, was eminently qualified to produce its own fine furniture of highly sophisticated designs, was made in 1953 with the publication of my *Directory of Antique Furniture*. This included a section with almost two hundred of such designs that were then recognizable as *Irish* to me and to a number of other professionals also interested in discouraging a continued designation of all such masterpieces as *English*, a deceptive term now increasingly questioned by the more knowledgeable of American collectors.

That publication received an unusually large and wide distribution of some 100,000 copies over the following decades, during which I undertook the first researches ever to have *scientifically* investigated the subject of British furniture as a whole, and of Irish furniture in particular. Through those extensive and minutely detailed comparative studies I was finally able to distinguish as Dublin furniture the thousands of such unrecognized capital city masterpieces arbitrarily misrepresented as *English* throughout the literature and in every leading British and American museum.

Such a limited presentation had no effect whatsoever toward bringing about a desired change in the *status quo*. The more staple Dublin productions continued to be exhibited and published as *English*, and with increasing frequency the more lavishly shaped, inlaid, and ormolu-mounted Dublin extravaganzas were blindly accepted, exhibited, and published with museum sponsorships as *Made in London* by craftsmen whose working designs and techniques were, still are, and will always continue to be entirely unknown.

Thus it was obvious that only through more amply represented sequences of Dublin designs, and more comprehensive displays of all Dublin style developments, would it ever become possible to overcome the persistent dilettantism of all such British lay experts as those who have nevertheless been entrusted with the informing of collectors, students of design, and the public in general.

Since most of my former colleagues who had been engaged in the Dublin trade prior to and during the turn of the nineteenth century were no longer available, our aims were made known to a number of presently active members of the British Antique Dealers' Association and the National Antique and Art Dealers Association of America. A gratifying selection of photographs to be checked out by my comparative proving methods was contributed by such internationally respected professional authorities as Michel

Trevor Venis (Trevor, London); Reginald Lumb (Charles Lumb and Sons, Harrogate); F. Roy Stamp (Biggs of Maidenhead); G. H. Holland (Asprey and Company, London); M. F. B. Hanson (Jeremy, London); Jack Treleaven (Needham's Antiques, New York); Joel Wolff (J. J. Wolff, New York); and Robert Samuels, Jr. (French and Company, New York).

The generous response of these knowledgeable and most ethical professionals has been of inestimable value in compiling three separate volumes, presenting a full and continuous documentation of all Dublin style developments in furniture and looking glasses throughout the eighteenth and early nineteenth century.

With more than five times the number of incontestable Dublin examples than those previously shown, arranged for easy comparisons and reference purposes, it may now be recognized that such an illusory term as *English* can no longer be sanctioned in respect to such obviously un-English productions. Then just as soon as the deceptive museum labels are changed, leading British and American professional authorities will be able to act accordingly without any break in their amicable relations with museum directors. They will then be entirely free to acknowledge the undeniable capital city status of their most distinguished, imaginatively designed and exceptionally decorative Dublin treasures that, to American collectors in particular, have been held in higher esteem than any of the relatively few London masterpieces that—as clearly brought out by both Herbert Cescinsky and R. W. Symonds, the two most widely recognized English authorities—were *made principally for royalty and the nobility,* and have seldom been permitted to reach the open market.

Foreword

W HEN THE COLLECTING of Old English Furniture came into vogue during the later decades of the nineteenth century, American demands could not be met in the London market. Alternate sources of supply were found in Dublin and in direct dealing with the owners of old, handsomely furnished Irish residences. One of the most successfully established of the first American traders to discover this treasure trove of what eventually came to be accepted as *English* rather than as *Irish* furniture, was Daniel Farr, who was well on in years when, in the 1940s, I had the good fortune to be able to talk with him about that unrecognized trade.

Members of British society were also aware that London had little or nothing of interest to them in the way of antique Queen Anne and Georgian furniture durng those years, and they too flocked to Ireland, especially during the annual Dublin Social Seasons. The Dublin market was also most appropriate for the refurbishing of old English residences that originally had been supplied with her furniture and looking glasses, along with chandelieres and other glasswares from Waterford—both ports being free of the exorbitant excise taxes imposed on all forms of English glass.

Since the original furnishings of old English residences were not so readily obtainable for the first loan exhibitions of Old English Furniture at the turn of the nineteenth century, these were provided with unrecognized Dublin masterpieces, such as those brought over from Ireland by Sir Spencer Ponsonby Fane and his bride when moving into Brympton D'Enercy, in Somerset. Such exhibits were then illustrated in the first books on the subject of *Old English Furniture*, by Constance Simon and by Percy Macquoid.

By the 1920s the mounting confusion had reached a point where an American museum curator claimed it to be "an established fact that much of the fine furniture used in Ireland was made in England" (*Metropolitan Museum Bulletin*, Vol. 24 (1929): 299). This was despite the established fact that *none* of the fine furniture made in England (*i.e.* London) was ever used in Ireland prior to modern times, while *much* of the high-quality furniture made in Dublin was readily delivered to many important residences in England, as well as to others in Scotland and Wales.

During the 1940s and 1950s Dublin was still the only great capital in Europe of whose *high quality* furniture nothing was known. In fact, Dublin has been continuously ignored to this day by all British literary and museum authorities claiming expertise in "Old English Furniture." Two of the leading English writers on both English and Irish furniture, Ralph Edwards and Margaret Jourdain, joined forces to bring out the first book particularly concerned with the work of London craftsmen: *Georgian Cabinet-Makers* (London, 1944, 1946, 1955). Neither was aware of the Irish capital's existence as a most important center in the production of high-quality furniture for its citizens and for export.

Of real value to these researches, however, their note on "T. [*sic*] CHANNON Fl. *circa*

1754" gives proof positive, aside from that obvious through Designs, of the poorly contrived and naïvely accepted CHANNON HOAX, *vide post*. On the other hand, their attention to PETER LANGLOIS "Worked in England, *Circa* 1760-1770," has been purposefully misinterpreted. Langlois' speciality of "inlaying in the politest manner with brass and tortoiseshell" has been misrepresented as having relevance to the entirely unrelated inlays of naturally colored and artificially tinted wood veneers appearing in Dublin's great Hepplewhite and Sheraton marquetry commodes and cabinets of *circa* 1770-1800. Their characteristic marquetry inlays of scrolling stems of rose leaves and blossoms are shown here in Pl 154, 155, 157, 159, 160, 163, 181, 183, 184.

Responsibility for accepting, sustaining and increasing the general confusion over "Old English Furniture" (in reality Dublin vis-à-vis London furniture) must be laid to the enthusiastic but superficial investigative activities of literary and museum authorities who have followed the general systematic research procedures *only* in respect to the more limited and less fanciful bona fide London productions. Especially blameworthy are those who in the 1960s and 1970s changed from their former espousal of the term "English," to claim that more recent importations into the London antique market had been made in London by little-known or entirely unknown London artisans.

To cite but one recent publication in which such inaccuracies have been stated: *The History of Furniture*, London and New York, 1976. On page 130 of this large, handsome and most impressive volume is a color illustration of the Victoria and Albert Museum's much publicized Dublin commode-form library table. The caption reads:

> This writing and dressing table is almost unique in English furniture for the profusion of its gilt-bronze Rococo mounts and the complicated swellings and recessions of the bodywork. It is attributed to John Channon, who worked in St. Martin's Lane specializing in furniture inlaid with brass, and was made during the 1740s. There is obvious German influence in both the shape and ornamentation, but the interpretation of Rococo design has become rather confused. Note the inclusion of dolphins at the bottom centre.

The book's dust jacket features "A rosewood chair, made in England about 1753 by John Channon." In this the arm terminals and their supports are whorled together in a characteristic Dublin fashion that was never duplicated in London, or in any other city of the western world. Two settees and two armchairs incorporating this typical Dublin structural feature are illustrated, 67, 68, 72 and 87, in my *Directory of Queen Anne, Early Georgian and Chippendale Furniture*.

On page 132 another color illustration is of an unmistakably distinctive Dublin marquetry serpentine-bombé commode, elaborately mounted in ormolu. (*Vide* Pl 154.) The description reads:

> "Pierre Langlois made this marquetry commode in England in about 1760. The carcase is made of pine in the English tradition (whereas the best French carcase-work was of oak), but a marble top to a commode is unusual in England." (*Vide* p. 43.)

Among the other Dublin masterpieces included in that *History*, page 128, is the famous Badminton House bedstead, there claimed as "made for the Duke of Beaufort in about 1752 by the Linnels." Also on page 80 is a Dublin Georgian cabinet of the type generally mistaken as *Charles II*, and as supposedly made somewhere in England. This is described as a

"Dutch lacquer cabinet, with door panels and drawers decorated with flower paintings, and the originally carved and gilded stand. The Dutch love of flowers extended to furniture as much as to painting, and this type of decoration soon became as popular as the oriental scenes on earlier lacquer pieces. The stand is exceptionally richly carved with figures emerging from a background of thick acanthus foliage in the style of Quellin and Grinling Gibbons." [!]

The overwhelming profusion of misinformation contained in those lengthy captions will bear witness to the great need for a first *scientific English study* of furniture designs actually carried out in London, *versus* those that were produced in the sister capital of Dublin. That need is also emphasized in a review of the pieces selected by Edwards and Jourdain for illustrating their work on *Georgian Cabinet-Makers*. Where these had been made for famous buildings such as Buckingham Palace, Windsor Castle, Hampton Court Castle, etc. the authors were on safe ground. But with pieces they represented as "Attributed to," or "Probably by William Vile, Thomas Chippendale," etc., more often than not they had again been swayed by the high quality, or conspicuously high quality of typical Dublin masterpieces.

The great productivity of the Irish capital in relation to that of London is also indicated by the scarcity of *LONDON* labels, in contrast to the overwhelming abundance of *ENGLISH* labels in all leading British and American museums. Since the two capital cities were also the only two metropolitan furniture-producing centers in the entirety of the British Isles, it must inevitably follow that all masterpieces of fine metropolitan designs and construction that cannot be accurately assigned to London were therefore designed and executed in the sister capital of Dublin.

Corrections at this late date will require not only more disciplined studies of Queen Anne and Georgian designs that were *NOT* produced in London, but also those that were *NOT* produced in any of the Continental furniture centers. Of all the European countries that have been mistakenly associated with the production of unrecognized Dublin furniture and looking glasses, Holland has been the one most frequently guessed at by museum and auction experts. Such guesses have obviously been made by those with no understanding of the designs actually carried out in that country, or of the tectonic methods employed there in accordance with strict governmental regulations.

As a recent instance, a typical Dublin George II walnut tray-top table appeared as lot 1674 in *The Benjamin Sonnenberg Collection*, sold in June of 1979. In the catalogue of the sale this was described as "Dutch, *circa* 1720." As a less frequent misrepresentation, a Chinese-Chippendale wall mirror with dragon finials matching those of the famous Badminton House bedstead and virtually *en suite* with it, has for many years been exhibited in the same museum as *German*.

Similar oversights have also resulted from beliefs, even by veteran professionals, that some of the most palatial masterpieces of Dublin furniture must be English because they are so fine, both in their highly sophisticated designs and their exceptionally skilled ornamental treatments. Among the first London antique dealers to advertise their stocks of "Old English Furniture" early in the present century, Moss Harris became internationally known for his generously illustrated catalogues. In one he showed an especially ornate cabinet, so unbelievably fabulous in its design and ornamental details that it was captioned as a *Louis XIV* example "Made in France, Probably for the Russian Market." This was a rare and most distinguished Dublin production of such magnificence that should it reappear in the London antique market today it would no doubt be recognized by the English licensing authorities as an Item of National Interest. As such it would then not be allowed to leave its supposed *Country of Origin.* On further recognition by museum furniture historians as another of the highly publicized series of Dublin extravaganzas promoted and accepted as "Made in London by John Channon," it might then be exhibited with a related but less ostentatious cabinet-on-stand already installed and mislabeled in the Victoria and Albert Museum.

As more and more of such stupendous Dublin creations have appeared in the London and New York antique markets, their illustration in recent books, periodicals, museum bulletins, and auction catalogues have added to the prestige, aesthetic appreciation, and value of others that have followed. Resulting auction and retail prices have achieved record figures, higher by far than those paid for any of the relatively few bona fide London pieces that have ever been permitted to enter the open market. (*Vide* caption of 325.)

A general enlightenment at this time of the difference between Dublin and London designs, no matter how essential and desirable to the more ethical members of the antique profession (while not to others), cannot be initiated within that circle. It would be most imprudent, to say the least, for any professional still actively engaged in the "Old English Furniture" business to challenge the existing prejudicial system of museum classification, which relies on unprofessional judgments and groundless assumptions. The more knowing professionals are thus obliged to follow those forced classifications rather than embarrass present-day authorities who persist in continuing the untenable policy of ignoring Dublin as the real source of most high-quality Queen Anne and Georgian seat furniture, cabinetwork, and looking glasses.

Dublin's Versatile Designers and Ornamentalists

Today museum personnel and lay writers still continue the myth of Dublin's nonexistence as a manufacturing center of first importance in the production of fine Queen Anne and Georgian furniture; it should nevertheless be obvious to the better informed collectors, as it is to the more knowledgeable members of the antique profession, that the subject of so-called Old English Furniture has yet to receive any scientific, systematic, or even moderately serious attention from these widely accepted authorities.

The fact that such masterpieces are clearly representative of metropolitan designs and technological accomplishments and must therefore be accredited to one or the other of the only two former metropolitan furniture producing centers in the whole of the British Isles: either London or Dublin, has had no meaning to these particular furniture enthusiasts. Since they have been unable to distinguish between the two separate and distinct schools of design, all such capital city productions that cannot be correctly associated with London origins have been arbitrarily designated as English, or as supposedly made in some nonexistent metropolitan furniture center of the provinces. As a result, most examples of Queen Anne and Georgian furniture and looking glasses that are presently exhibited in English and American museums have been deprived of their capital city status; they have as well had their true source of production still carelessly misrepresented throughout these educational institutions and in the museum bulletins and other publications.

When such supplies were first sought by American dealers during the later decades of the nineteenth century they found that, contrary to their expectations, London was unable to meet their demands; this situation is confirmed by illustrated articles and advertisements in the earliest issues of *The Connoisseur* magazine. Instead, it was discovered that an alternate source existed, one that had been and continued to be patronized by members of the British aristocracy. Thus Lord St. Oswald, in adding to the original furnishing of Nostel Priory about 1883, acquired various articles of Dublin seat furniture, which on the basis of their high quality have since been "authoritatively" assigned to Chippendale;* while Lady Randolph Churchill, during her Ireland years (1877-1881) was able to obtain choice pieces from ancestral homes in her rounds of the Dublin antique shops.**

When furniture obtained from those same ancestral homes was received in America and shortly thereafter in England, these importations were described as English by the early traders of both countries. With the unquestioning acceptance of that tongue-in-cheek designation by contemporary and later museum officials and writers in general, the term

---

*Edwards & Jourdain, *Georgian Cabinet-Makers*, 1955, p 70.
**Ralph G. Martin, *Jennie*, 1969.

has also gone unquestioned by present day collectors. The most important selections of such "Old English Furniture" in New York City, prior to and after the turn of the nineteenth century, were those acquired by Daniel Farr, who stopped going to Ireland in 1903, for by that time he was able to obtain the same high quality merchandise more conveniently in London. Aside from calling everything English, none of the international importers concerned themselves with the actual source of such pieces, or with the fact that since they obviously conformed with London in technological advances they would also accord with those of the sister capital.

Other shipments of Dublin furniture arriving in America during and just after the turn of the nineteenth century included those received by Karl Freund, then a popular New York City dealer and decorator. These were made up of his selections from the stocks of Irish dealers and from private residences throughout the country, and were intended for homes he had been commissioned to furnish and for the auction sales held in his behalf. Typical of other auctions at that time was "A Notable Collection of English Furniture" sold at The American Art Galleries, Madison Square South, New York, in December of 1910. Catalogued by Luke Vincent Lockwood, the collection was comprised mainly of Dublin examples and Irish provincial pieces, with a few items that Lockwood failed to recognize as similarly designed but genuinely American-made productions. Except for a number of clocks, the only English furniture in the entire collection was a fine London window seat (No. 253 in the catalogue) that has recently been illustrated in an English magazine advertisement as a known and wanted example after a design by Robert Adam.

In 1926 the Leverhulme Collection was sent here for auction following the famous trial in England over its many fraudulent pieces. Herbert Cescinsky, who had been accepted as an expert in that trial, was brought over to catalogue the collection. In doing so he described both fraudulent pieces and modern reproductions as genuine eighteenth-century examples, in one instance hesitantly noting a brand new Tottenham Court Road sofa table, in perfect condition, as having been "Restored." Of the genuine pieces, one of the most outstanding Dublin items was a tall brass-inlaid architectural writing cabinet. This was later illustrated and described by R. W. Symonds (*Country Life*, May 7, 1948 and January 13, 1950) as another "tour de force of the English cabinet-maker's craft." Subsequently it has been included with other Dublin masterpieces claimed as the work of a provincially trained English craftsman, John Channon, unknown to Symonds or to Edwards and Jourdain, but for whom a London working address has recently been discovered. *(Vide post.)*

A surprising lack of investigative interest in respect to the productive capacity of the Irish capital was evident after searches made in Ireland for R. W. Symonds could discover no evidence of English furniture ever being received in that country prior to modern times. Then, after a long career as the leading authority on Old English Furniture, apparently with some professional enlightenment, he was finally moved to advise his followers, in a magazine article, that

"if a piece is known to have come out of Ireland it is accepted as having been made there."

In this he still failed to recognize the existence of Dublin as the only possible native source of fine metropolitan designs and craftsmanship, just as he never was able to realize that London was the only such production center in the whole of Great Britain. Nor was he ever able to correct the unbroken flood of mistakes he had made, and continued to make, in publishing many hundreds of Dublin masterpieces as of "English," "North Country," or even as of "London" origins.

The essence of scientific research in the field of antique furniture is the comparative proving method followed in these studies: the juxtaposing of items—i.e. photographs and halftones—to establish similarities and dissimilarities. This is the system obviously followed by English museum and literary experts solely in regard to the relatively few historic, or otherwise safely documented London productions. The following illustrations have been selected with a view toward maintaining continuities in which, as far as possible here, one sequence of designs serves in proving or confirming the related developments in another.

For instance, stools, chairs, and settees are grouped together for comparison with tables of various types and other related cabinet pieces. Ornamental treatments such as those accomplished through inlays or painted decorations are also grouped together as far as possible, with special attention to tables, commodes, and cabinets displaying various distinctive features that are important in the proving or confirming of many outstanding Dublin productions. Rather than indulging in tedious running textual commentaries on such characteristic forms and decorative treatments, comparisons are suggested in many of the captions.

One of the most distinctive features of Dublin vis-à-vis London seat furniture is the occasional use of inversive cable fluting, in which the reeds drop rather than rise within the flutings of square legs (65, 74), round legs (97), or even in modified cabriole legs (57). Incidentally, the slipper chair (97), formerly believed to be American, is of a heart-and-shield pattern obviously brought over to Philadelphia by a Dublin-trained craftsman. The same inversive use of cable fluting may also be seen in the Dublin-Hepplewhite urn stand (147) and card table (174), and in the sideboard (237). Other designs are distinguished by an inversive use of gadrooning, as in the Dublin-Hepplewhite card table (25), contrasting with the more correct use in (26); both examples show the reduced scale of such edgings in comparison with those of earlier years. The delicate edging of the apron in (24) is hardly perceptible as regular gadrooning.

During the early years of these first scientific researches to be concentrated on Old *British* Furniture, by proving those two particular idiosyncrasies to be characteristic of certain Dublin craftsmen, the few dozen chairs and tables in which they appeared enabled me, through their overall designs, to identify still other examples with neither cable fluting nor gadrooning, and thus to multiply my findings to an appreciable extent by the late 1950s.

Among the Dublin productions that are easily determined by their structural forms are those chairs, stools and settees that have come to be accepted as of "French-Hepplewhite" designs (1-18). Rather than resembling Parisian or other French metropolitan examples, they are more closely akin to German, Danish and other Continental versions of transitional Louis XV-Louis XVI designs. Once their most distinctive Dublin-Hepplewhite forms and details are recognized as such, similar effects will be noticed in tables of various sorts (19-28) and in larger pieces.

No closely similar designs were produced in London. Actually, from the number of these distinctive Dublin armchairs remaining today it appears that they were manufactured in far greater quantities than any armchairs simultaneously produced in the English capital.

This would also seem credible according to the contemporary report of a French visitor who was surprised to find that

> "Londoners have scarce any arm-chairs in their apartments . . . they are satisfied with the common ones."

As to painted decorations, probably a greater variety of designs in seat furniture were so treated in Dublin during the late eighteenth and early nineteenth century than in any other capital of Europe. Trophies, urns, bowknots, paterae, etc. were often combined with the usual floral and vine treatments, sometimes also with the introduction of figural subjects. Such effects were repeated in tables, commodes, and cabinets. In fact, a characteristic black-and-gold armchair of the general type illustrated here (137-141) featured a back panel with exactly the same representation of cherubs flanking pairs of cupids with a goat, as that repeated in the frieze panel of the secretary-cabinet (373).

Many of the floral and figural subjects that are so characteristic of the Dublin school of decorative painting, *circa* 1780-1820, have appeared in seat furniture and cabinet pieces that have been published as English; such decorations are represented as *"by," "attributed to,"* or *"in the style of Angelica Kauffmann"* (*Vide* Pl 153, 173, 177, 191). Although she executed murals in Ireland (Plate 200), it is unlikely that she did any painting of furniture while there except on such an occasion as that when she is supposed to have decorated the tops of a pair of tables for Lord Ely, leaving it for him to have a number of others marbelized. She left the British Isles for good in 1782.

The typical Dublin painted decoration on the top surface of the gilded console table (Plate 147) served in confirming the true origin of the armchair *en suite* (Ill 33). Without that proof it would have been impossible to disprove the pure German design of the chair itself and to show it here as obviously made by an emigré joiner, probably in his own shop.

In the simplicity of their serpentine forms, apron shapings, and inlays, the typical Dublin-Hepplewhite commodes (29 and 258) are just as readily identifiable as others that are further distinguished by distinctive panel bandings (257), the more reserved marquetry decorations (254, 333, 334), lacquer work (30), or the grand marquetry serpentine-bombé commodes elaborately mounted in ormolu (325, 326). The Louis XVI-type handles of (29) and (258) are accompanied by side handles of lion's heads linked by knobbed bails, as in the Late Chippendale double chest-of-drawers (376); these same handles are also found on contemporary work of pure Regency designs.

The ormolu stile capitals of the lacquer commode (30) and the cabinet combining both marquetry and parquetry panels (363) were copied from a pattern favored by German marquetry workers employed in Paris but not accepted into the guild of *maitres ébénistes.* Their forms and marquetry treatments often followed those of Joseph Schmitz. That particular stile mount is thus found on unsigned Parisian marquetry commodes dating from *circa* 1770. In Dublin productions it is often combined with an ormolu gadrooned molding around the top edge of commodes and cabinets as in (30) and (363) (*cf* 347, 348). Consequently its adoption in Dublin is more safely determined as occurring between 1775 and 1800. Similar stile treatments combined with handles and escutcheons in the rococo taste (but sometimes with side handles of the Late Chippendale-Regency pattern appearing in [29, 258, 376]) have led to Hepplewhite commodes of forms such as (29 and 258) being mistakenly classified as Chippendale examples.

Since they ignore the existence of Dublin and therefore of its ability to produce its own important Hepplewhite ormolu-mounted marquetry serpentine-bombé commodes (such as 325 and 326), English authorities are completely unaware of the true *circa* dates that should be associated with their manufacture. Regardless of their Hepplewhite marquetry patterns, their rococo mounts invariably lead to their being dated as *circa* 1760—to fit the date of Pierre Langlois' return to Paris, rather than as *circa* 1770 and later.

Edwards and Jourdain were even further off the mark in their description (*op cit* p. 102)

of "a pair of fine serpentine-fronted mahogany commodes, *c.* 1760, with elaborate brass rococo handles" bearing the trade label of MACK, WILLIAMS and GIBTON, a firm they noted as "Fl. *circa* 1760, at 39 Stratford Street, Dublin."

As leading English researchists they ignored the possibility of obtaining further information in that capital; and they took no particular notice of the fact that the firm was able to announce itself as "Upholsterers and Cabinet Makers to His Majesty," although they could not mention a similar honor as being advertised by any London firm.

In answer to my own inquiry, John Teahan in the National Museum of Ireland responded:

"John Mack, cabinet maker, had an address at 188 Abbey Street in 1785. In the period 1794-1800 he also had an address at 39 Stafford Street. Soon after this time he began to work in partnership with another cabinet maker called Gibton and they were listed at the same addresses in 1805 and 1810. Around this time they were joined by another cabinet maker called Williams. Mack, Williams and Gibton were listed together at 39 Stafford Street from 1815 to 1825."

Thus the pair of commodes with elaborate brass rococo handles could not have been made before 1815.

The pair of marquetry commodes in palisander, olivewood and holly (Pl 156-157) attests to the unusual versatility of Dublin cabinetmakers in their choice of rare woods, as well as the variety of their marquetry patterns and of their ormolu mounts and edgings. When this pair passed through my hands, prior to 1952, I was not acquainted with the excellence of Dublin designs and working skills; I could not bring myself to believe they were *Irish* despite the fact that they had come out of Castle Moyle, in County Kerry; and of course I catalogued them as *English*, also not knowing that any similar skills would have been available only in London. One of another pair with the same mounts and edgings, but in plain mahogany is illustrated in Jourdain and Rose, *English Furniture: the Georgian Period,* p. 113, as "From Fawley Court, Henly-on-Thames"; and a tall chest-of-drawers with matching ormolu work surmounted by fret-pierced open shelves, is illustrated in the *Dictionary of English Furniture,* Vol. 1, p. 141.

The breakfront marquetry commode displaying such a wealth of ornamental details and materials plate 160, is one of the numerous unpublicized Dublin masterpieces specially made for old residences throughout Great Britain, in this instance for St. Giles House, Dorset, in the south rather than the west of England. In the following decorated lacquer example plate 161, the stile mounts and edgings contrast with the plainness of the valanced apron, but such diversities do appear in even the most elaborate of Dublin productions.

The Sheraton bonheur du jour (162) shows a more complete use of holly and a pair of

Adamesque loose-ring handles. Just as rococo handles appear on Dublin-Hepplewhite pieces as well as on those of Chippendale and Late Chippendale designs, these circular handles, centering classic urns with flanking ram's heads, are found on pieces of Sheraton and Regency designs (*vide* 244, 252).

It would have been impossible to continue disregarding Dublin's productivity if the handle patterns of the very few pieces that have been acknowledged as originating in Ireland as a whole had been allowed to play a part in English comparative studies such as those that have concentrated only on documented London productions. Had the leading English writer of past decades, R. W. Symonds, made such a study, he would not have aided in promoting the Channon Hoax, *(vide post)*, by declaring that one of the most typical of Dublin rococo handles (*vide* Macquoid's *Age of Mahogany*, Fig 128; *Country Life*, January 13, 1950; *Leeds Art Calendar*, No. 39, Fig 1-3) had been "specially made in Paris" for one of the commodes subsequently promoted, with museum endorsements, as "Made in London by John Channon."

Other easily recognizable rococo handles appear on the commode (255), and in (257), with its distinctive stile edgings treated as those in (333). Louis XVI-type handles are shown in (249), a representative Dublin-Hepplewhite form, and in (290), a Late Georgian chest-on-chest in which the base is of a pure Chippendale design. Perhaps the most unmistakable of all the late handle patterns is the one that adds distinction to even such superlative satinwood creations as (355, 368 and 372).

It is just as unlikely that Dublin handles would be exported to London as it is that London handles would be ordered from faraway Dublin; however, it appears that handles of patterns such as those shown in (238, 277, 278, 169 and 376) were conveniently delivered from Dublin directly across the Irish Sea to Lancaster. This port town became the second and only other English furniture center to develop outside London during the eighteenth century because of the presence there of the much touted Gillow factory. According to a census taken early in the following years, by 1815 Lancaster had achieved a population of 3,050.

A favorite Regency star-and-knob drawer pull (181, 185, 191) was helpful in determining a large number of Dublin sofa tables. Confirmations were also obtained through the combination of ormolu pearl moldings, top edging and *sabots* or toe caps of (181); and the lower die mount of (185), which appeared on a sofa table and a saber-leg side chair owned by Sir Spencer Ponsonby Fane.

The brass-inlaid sofa table (188) has been carefully recorded as having been "Made in 1816 for Princess Charlotte," but in keeping with customary procedure, attention has not been drawn to the fact that this was another instance of royal patronage favoring the designs of Dublin cabinetmakers over those available in London. The patterns of the brass inlays (along with those of 182, 189, 193, 194, and 245) were all instrumental in proving many other Dublin productions.

Inkwork decorations as in the sofa table (187) are illustrative of the resourcefulness and creative ability of the Dublin ornamentalists during the turn of the eighteenth century. In this table, and in the dwarf cabinets (273 and 275), the effects, especially of the multiple borders, are reminiscent of the somewhat similar decorations in ivory-surfaced furnishings received from India during the early years of the nineteenth century. A similar bordering effect, in an otherwise plain sofa table, is illustrated in Jourdain and Rose, *English Furniture: the Georgian Period*, p. 78.

Egyptian terms as in the inkwork piece (273) are repeated in the secretaire (299), in which the sides of the drop-front writing drawer do not extend in the regular shaping (as in 276, 279, 280, 293, 296, 297 and 304), but are indented above the quadrant catch. This is a treatment found only in Dublin cabinetwork of very high quality. Egyptian terms are also shown here in (179) and in Margaret Jourdain, *Regency Furniture*, Fig 222, a dressing table owned by the Duke of Wellington.

The card table (195) is one of a pair that was sold as "The finest New England pedestal tables known"; (196) was sold as a "New York, N.Y." masterpiece; although ormolu mounts such as those of both (196 and 197) are generally considered as justification for attributing such pieces to the French *ébéniste* Honoré Lannuier, who worked in New York, (197) was routinely sold as *English*.

A label of "Mack, Williams and Gibton" with their address given only as "39 Stafford Street," on a Georgian tripod dumbwaiter illustrated in the revised edition of the *Dictionary of English Furniture*, Vol. 1, p. 97, provided the first clue to many other late pieces with ogival tripods having raised pad feet (as in 203, 204, 205, and 206). Knowing that over 95 percent of all tripod pieces with dished or piecrust trays had been made in Dublin rather than London, and that outside of that one English city there were no others to which enquiries might rationally be addressed, I obtained the previously noted evidence, (*vide* p. 36), that the *Dictionary* dumbwaiter was not made *circa* 1760, but over a half-century later. A similarly based dumbwaiter with Chippendale fret piercing and Regency ormolu gallery is illustrated in Jourdain and Rose, *English Furniture: the Georgian Period*, p. 153.

Late Chippendale furniture has often perplexed even the most experienced of antique dealers. For instance, when Sheraton drum tables (such as 214) or dining tables appear with ogival tripods terminating either in pad or claw-and-ball feet, they have also been mistakenly classified as Chippendale. The safest terminology would be George III, or just Georgian. It should also be realized that a persistent use of the seemingly earliest possible *circa* dates is apt to lead to the greatest possibility of errors. In publications by accepted authorities this may leave such mistakes as generally unnecessary but nevertheless permanent records of their shortcomings.

Dublin bandings, borders and other inlays that are less distinctive than marquetry patterns are too numerous and diverse to be dealt with in any but an encyclopedic coverage of those particular means of artistic expression. The covering of such techniques in any detail now would receive no more attention than it has received in the past. Then, too, without photographic magnification, one cannot easily see that a checkered link-chain banding, such as that of the chest-of-drawers with Chippendale-type bracket feet is repeated in another of more typical Dublin-Hepplewhite design (257). It is easier to see that the panel bandings of (266, 267, 268, 269, 282, 283 and 288), with or without the same dottings, are obviously of one particular school of design, but it may not be possible to see in the halftone illustrations that all are composed of five alternating light-and-dark-wood stringing lines.

Broader surface treatments are more easily recognizable. Of these, one of the most characteristic is the Dublin use of veneer surfaces of fine exotics such as satinwood, mahogany, and especially sabicu, framed by crossetted panel borders, as shown in one of the typical Dublin clock-cabinets (298). Similarly treated and similarly varied panels of sabicu appear in a small secretaire illustrated in the *Dictionary of English Furniture*, Fig 56;

and also in an advertised dwarf cabinet of sideboard length, obviously designed to serve such a dining-room purpose.

Some of these popular clock-cabinets combine Hepplewhite and Sheraton features; while in one of the same general Regency design as (298) the crossetted door panels, again of sabicu, are inset with oval figural panels of jasperware. The astragals, stepped cresting, and finials of the dining room cabinet (375) should be compared with the presently illustrated clock-cabinet, which probably was also intended for dining-room use.

The difference between this particular Dublin clock-cabinet (298) and those previously entering the market is that all of such clock dials originally had been unmarked, while in this particular instance an inscription had been added: "Weekes' Museum Tichborne Street." That legend has been accepted by leading English authorities as indicating that this individual clock-cabinet (and a series of at least ten others, now accepted in museum circles as "the Weekes' cabinets,") had originated in London, rather than Dublin. With those unquestioning acceptances, no thought has been given to the fact that no museum would ever have had its name and street address marked on the front of any item displayed within its own premises. Furthermore, the items acquired by Weekes' Museum were intended to "exhibit the powers of mechanism." Had it indeed been considered feasible for the wind-up spring movement of a clock to serve that purpose, there were innumerable larger and far more powerful clocks ready at hand in London, without resorting to one with a very ordinary movement encased in a large, space consuming, and costly housing.

An even greater absurdity was overlooked when still another in this series of matching clock-cabinets came into the London antique market with the very same inscription also added to its clock face (*vide* my book on *The More Significant Regency Furniture*, 52). Although it could hardly be overlooked that this was carrying things a bit too far, no questions were raised in museum circles over the absurdity of supposedly exhibiting two or more such cabinets in any single museum, either side by side or otherwise. In carrying out the Channon Hoax one inscribed but undated brass plate was removed and replaced by two brass plates both inscribed and dated 1740. In this other attempt at chicanery another false inscription, added to one clock face and later repeated on at least one other dial, is evidence pointing only to importation by the same overly self-confident London entrepreneur.

In a *Connoisseur* article of May 1971, "Some Weekes' cabinets reconsidered," Christopher Gilbert published a large group of such examples, along with other Dublin cabinetwork displaying the same decorative treatments that supposedly proved the London origins of all. Especially identifying are the panel inlays, *pieds en toupie* (as here 268, 269, 272), the patterns of bail, and *ajouré* patera handles, as well as those of ormolu galleries (such as in 283) surmounting some of the lower pieces.

Failure to recognize such distinctive features and details as *uncharacteristic* of London work can only detract from the assumed expertise of English furniture historians. After all, no one can have a true, unprejudiced understanding of Georgian furniture as a whole, while at the same time denying the very real presence of Dublin as the third-largest capital city furniture center of the eighteenth century.

As to Dublin's great marquetry furniture, it cannot be emphasized too strongly that the two widely publicized commodes (325 and 326) have absolutely nothing in common with any London Chippendale commodes of *circa* 1760-1770, or with any London commodes that have been associated with similar *circa* dates and classified as Hepplewhite. In such promotions museum authorities are prone to forget that Hepplewhite's *Cabinet-makers' and Upholsterers' Guide* was not first published until 1788. Nor could such fine marquetry work have been accomplished by the French revivalist of Andre Charles Boulle's inlaid decorations in tortoiseshell and metal. Indeed, Pierre Langlois was working in Paris at the time of their production, possibly as the "Pierre-Eloi Langlois" who in 1773 was accepted as a master in the Parisian *chair*-makers' guild (*vide* also p 22-24).

When in 1908 Percy Macquoid published his *Age of Satinwood* he illustrated a 'commode' similar to (337) as Irish. That illustration was removed and included in a special proving file of inlaid furniture believed to be Irish, but still not verified. It was not until Ralph Edwards, in a magazine article, published an inlaid commode at Welbeck Abbey as made for and billed to the Duke of Portland by William Moore of Dublin, in 1782, that every piece in that entire group was finally accepted, not just as *Irish*, but at long last as a Dublin masterpiece.

R. W. Symonds, a much later English writer, criticized Macquoid for not giving the sources of the furniture he had so liberally illustrated in his four *Ages of Old English Furniture*—this without realizing that neither Macquoid nor he himself would have been informed about any of the pieces either of them had published. Indeed the principal source of Symonds' illustrated pieces was one of the earliest and most avid English collectors of the present century, Percival Griffiths, who also would not have been informed about the original source of most of the furniture he acquired. Symonds himself had been kept in the dark by his favorite dealers, about the sources of their most recent importations, which he published for them without the slightest suspicion that they were not "English," or "North Country," productions. Nevertheless, when Percy Macquoid did in fact give sources in connection with such Dublin treasures as those descended in the DeLisle and Dudley family, their true origin went entirely unrecognized by Symonds.

English museum curators have never recognized the only practical system for determining the great differences between the designs of London furniture and looking glasses and those of her sister capital. This entails the systematic comparison of all possible photographs and halftone illustrations of British furniture appearing in books, periodicals, catalogues, etc. that have dealt with the subject of so-called Old English Furniture. Thus in writing about William Moore, Edwards and Jourdain were able to recognize only one piece in the whole of the Victoria and Albert Museum as another commode attributable to Moore on stylistic grounds, and a side-table formerly at Lismore Castle, County Waterford—this despite the large number of Moore-inlaid tea caddies and trays, center and side tables, chests-of-drawers, low and tall cabinets that were available to both authors in museums, dealers' stocks, and in private collections according to those readily identifiable examples that had already been illustrated in the literature.

Moore was exceptionally talented in devising his own distinctive stile inlays, paterae, frieze panels, and intricate top edgings, as well as his larger marquetry compositions; however, it appears that Moore's skills did not extend to those required in producing sideboard tables, pedestals, and urns such as those shown in plate 88. The inlays, however, are unmistakably his; apparently his artistic coöperation in that capacity was sought by other Dublin shop owners of even higher repute.

In comparison with the more usual plain or simply inlaid mahogany or satinwood cabinets and bookcases, those with marquetry or painted decorations (as 368-375) were often of unusual forms and incorporated novel structural features that set off those embellishments through which their identities are made clear. A highlight in the unwritten history of Dublin exportations of furniture and looking glasses, in connection with both British and American naval officers, sea captains and supercargoes, is the cabinet of "conspicuously high quality," (372) that was shipped to Naples, *circa* 1800, for presentation there by Admiral Viscount Horatio Nelson to Lady Hamilton, who had nursed him back to health after he lost an arm in the Battle of the Nile.

An early objective of these researches was the determination of those great houses in western and southern areas of England whose owners had found it more advantageous to obtain their best furniture and looking glasses from nearby Dublin, rather than from far removed London. Toward that end it soon became necessary to maintain a working list of such old residences with their names and those of the original or later owners alphabetically arranged; this has facilitated ready reference as more and more of such installations, along with Waterford chandelieres, have come to light in illustrations of the literature supposedly concentrated on "Old English Furniture." A more extended coverage was soon required, however, as old residences in other areas of England as well as in Scotland and Wales were also discovered to contain Dublin furniture. Finally it became advisable to include the names of more recent owners of such illustrated examples.

For possible assistance in further studies of the designs presented here (as well as those of other Dublin masterpieces that have been continuously published ever since the earliest 1900s, primarily as *English* but occasionally as *London* or even as *American* productions), that working list of past and present owners of the most imaginatively designed *British* furniture is included here.

English furniture of metropolitan designs and working techniques was produced principally for members of the royal family and the nobility, a point on which both Herbert Cescinsky and R. W. Symonds could both agree; very few of such examples have ever been permitted to enter the open market. Therefore this listing, along with the following presentations, should be of interest to private collectors and museums owning few if any safely documented London productions; it should help them to realize the full importance and true metropolitan character of those Dublin masterpieces that have been acquired and are presently exhibited merely as "English." They may also now appreciate the prestigious fellowship of owners, including members of the British royal family from the eighteenth and early nineteenth century, up until quite recent years (*vide* caption of 352) who have displayed the same discriminating taste in their own preferences for Queen Anne and Georgian masterpieces originating in Dublin, rather than London.

As a tailpiece a provincial chest-of-drawers plate 201 will indicate the futility of a hypothesis advanced by all accepted English "experts" on Irish furniture from R. W. Symonds to those of today, in which they have continuously maligned and misinterpreted Irish furniture in general as provincial. Since none of those experts has ever succeeded in recognizing the thoroughly distinctive differences between the capital city masterpieces of Ireland and those of England, they would be even less qualified to recognize any possibly discernable differences between truly provincial Irish examples and those produced in the even smaller towns of England.

The better furniture of Irish provincial towns does not exhibit the distinctive structural forms or ornamental treatments that are so characteristic of Dublin productions; while that of English provincial towns can be especially plain, conventional, and undeterminable. Thus without any clearly identifying features it would have been impossible to determine the real source of this representative provincial chest-of-drawers, except for its originally applied maker's label with Waterford address.

Incidentally, Waterford, with a population of 25,467, was considerably larger than the English town of Exeter, with a population of 17,398, according to census figures of the time. The latter figure should be of special significance to English furniture historians since their recently discovered John Channon (*vide* Index) received all of his training in that provincial town prior to 1737. He then worked in London, supposedly with immediate metropolitan skills of the highest order, supposedly equaling or surpassing those of the then leading London masters and also those finally achieved at about that time by the great Parisian *ébéniste*, Andre Charles Boulle. (*Vide* "The Channon family of Exeter and London, chair and cabinet makers," *Victoria and Albert Museum Bulletin*, April 1966.)

Addendum:
The Channon Hoax and other Obvious Deceptions

Decisive and undeniably conclusive evidence of the chicanery resulting in British museum acceptances of the so-called Channon Pieces ultimately rests upon the surprising discrepancies between two differing descriptions of the unorthodox metal plates on which those acceptances have been based.

According to Edwards and Jourdain (*Georgian Cabinet-Makers*, 1955, p 102):

"T. [sic] CHANNON, fecit, is inscribed on a brass plate attached to one of a pair of . . . bookcases . . . at Powderham Castle."

Contrarily, after the attention of John Hayward had been drawn to the same bookcases, he reported in the *Victoria and Albert Museum Bulletin* (April, 1966) that *Each* of the two Powderham bookcases

"is signed and dated on a brass plaque . . . The Signature J. CHANNON is in Gothic lettering and is accompanied by the date 1740."

Clearly, then, these two later brass plates, each inscribed with the date 1740, have now replaced the one former brass plate bearing no date.

Neither of those unprecedented uses of metal plates, intended for acceptances as original labelings, has ever been questioned by the usual lay authorities. Indeed one such museum curator has advised me that he considers the Hayward article to be both

"impressive and well researched . . . the inscribed tablet as genuine—there are a few [conspicuously unspecified] precedents."

Always when brass plates are to be attached to wood surfaces this also entails the use of brass screws. A set of four eighteenth-century screws of the size required for completing that bit of chicanery, especially in brass, would be most difficult if not impossible to obtain at the present time. Therefore without the professional training required to distinguish between antique and modern brass screws they, along with the two brass *plaques* for which they were supplied, should have been submitted by the museum experts for examination by a committee of the more knowledgeable and most ethical members of the British Antique Dealers Association.

Coincidentally, an even simpler form of inscriptive chicanery was employed in respect to the so-called Weekes' Museum Cabinets. When the first of these popular Dublin productions, embodying a plain summital clock of ordinary quality, came into the London market after its clock dial had been deceptively inscribed with the name and address of that old London institution, that freehand inscription was accepted in museum circles as pointing to a London origin for the entire piece.

With the general acceptance of that simple ruse, and with a fixed contempt for the reasoning powers of the usual lay authorities, the supplier then became so imprudent as to repeat the same stratagem on the dials of other similarly designed Dublin clock-cabinets. One of these is illustrated here (298) and in my *Directory of the Historic Cabinet Woods* (*vide* pages 49-50); and another has been held for my project on *The More Significant Regency Furniture.*

The unlikelihood as well as the impracticality of such multiple exhibits ever having been installed at the same time, or successively, in any one museum, with its own name and street address flaunted on every clock dial, has not been realized by any museum officials. For a *Connoisseur* article one such furniture historian has

> traced twelve, nearly identical models and a 'family' of over twenty items, all apparently from the same workshop."

Additional claims toward perpetuating the myths associated with supposedly London furniture have also recently been centered on the grandeur of Dublin's important Hepplewhite marquetry commodes (*vide* 325 and 326) displaying French, or actually Franco-Germanic influence in their forms, inlaid decorations, and the more reserved of their ormolu embellishments. Also with no possible justification, these effects have been claimed as representing the unknown work of a French *ébéniste*, Pierre Langlois. His trade card makes it emphatically clear, however, that rather than working in the usual natural and artificially-tinted wood veneers of London's marquetry decorations, he "inlaid in the politest manner with brass and tortoiseshell." In Mortimer's *Director* of 1765 he is also recorded as forming "all sorts of curious inlaid work . . . in the foreign taste, inlaid with tortoiseshell, brass, etc." *Vide Georgian Cabinet-Makers*, p. 103.

Thus no matter how expert Langlois may have been in such boullework decorations, it is preposterous even to suggest such an outmoded technique as in any way comparable to the marquetry treatments of Dublin's great serpentine-bombé commodes. Furthermore, the popularity of marquetry commodes such as those produced by John Cobb in 1772 for Corsham Court, by Thomas Chippendale in 1770 for Nostel Priory, or those developed in Dublin, also during the 1770s, does not coincide with the recorded stay of Langlois in London only during the 1760s.

There is very good reason for thus emphasizing the naiveté in which the so-called Channon, Weekes' Museum, and Langlois Pieces have been accepted and promoted by British museum authorities. If such misrepresentations are allowed to continue unchallenged, others are bound to follow until eventually the entirety of Dublin's unacknowledged but truly formidable production might well be similarly accepted, exhibited and published as also having originated in London.

Since British nonprofessional furniture experts of the last seventy-five years have persistently ignored the existence of Dublin as one of the greatest of all European capital city furniture centers, it will call for strict measures now to rectify this unprecendented situation. Initially, it must be realized at last in British museum circles that old English furniture of superior, museum, or capital city quality was not produced anywhere in that country outside of the capital city, for London was the only metropolitan furniture producing center there, just as Dublin was the only metropolitan furniture producing center in all Ireland.

When an international recognition of Dublin's former importance is finally achieved, American collectors will no longer outvie all others in paying record prices for their most highly valued but unrecognized Dublin masterpieces without having any perception of their true prestigious source. Then London labels will continue to appear in about the same meager proportion of those examples released from private English ownership and presented to or otherwise acquired by the more fortunate of British museums; while Dublin labels will be introduced in respect to the majority of Queen Anne and Georgian masterpieces that are now so widely and plentifully exhibited merely as undistinguished English examples.

Plates

PLATE 1

1 LATE CHIPPENDALE CARVED MAHOGANY STOOL.
Cf Percy Macquoid, *Age of Mahogany*, Fig. 186.
Courtesy of Needham's Antiques, Inc., New York City.

2 HEPPLEWHITE CARVED MAHOGANY STOOL

3 HEPPLEWHITE CARVED MAHOGANY WINDOW SEAT

PLATE 2

4 HEPPLEWHITE CARVED MAHOGANY ARMCHAIR

5 HEPPLEWHITE CARVED BEECH BERGERE

6 HEPPLEWHITE CARVED BEECH UPHOLSTERED SETTEE. *Cf* 7-8.

PLATE 3

7-8   HEPPLEWHITE PAIR/CARVED BEECH AND NEEDLEPOINT ARMCHAIRS. From the Countess of Kilmorey,
Monroe Park, County Down.

9.   HEPPLEWHITE CARVED BEECH AND NEEDLEPOINT SETTEE. *En suite.*

PLATE 4

10 HEPPLEWHITE MAHOGANY ARMCHAIR

11 HEPPLEWHITE CARVED MAHOGANY ARMCHAIR

12 HEPPLEWHITE CARVED MAHOGANY ARMCHAIR

13 HEPPLEWHITE CARVED MAHOGANY ARMCHAIR

PLATE 5

14 HEPPLEWHITE CARVED MAHOGANY ARMCHAIR

15 HEPPLEWHITE CARVED MAHOGANY ARMCHAIR

16 HEPPLEWHITE CARVED MAHOGANY SIDE CHAIR

17 HEPPLEWHITE CARVED AND PAINTED ARMCHAIR

PLATE 6

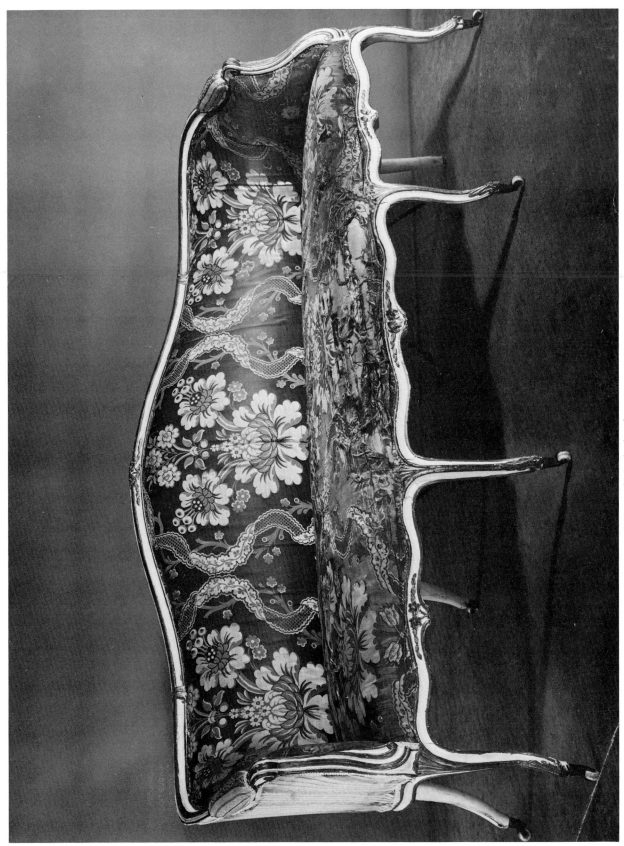

18 HEPPLEWHITE CARVED AND PAINTED SETTEE. Courtesy of Biggs of Maidenhead.

PLATE 7

19 HEPPLEWHITE INLAID MAHOGANY CELLARETTE

20 HEPPLEWHITE CARVED MAHOGANY URN STAND
WITH CHIPPENDALE OPEN-FRET GALLERY. *Vide* Fig. 4,
Dictionary of English Furniture.

21-22   PAIR HEPPLEWHITE WRITING AND DRESSING TABLES

PLATE 8

23 HEPPLEWHITE MAHOGANY PEMBROKE TABLE. From a Scottish collection.
Courtesy of Needham's Antiques, Inc., New York City.

24 HEPPLEWHITE CARVED MAHOGANY CARD TABLE. *Vide* also Macquoid & Edwards,
Dictionary of English Furniture, 3, 194; from Culzean Castle, Ayrshire.

PLATE 9

25 HEPPLEWHITE CARVED MAHOGANY CARD TABLE. With inverse gardrooning. Victoria & Albert Museum. Crown Copyright.

26 HEPPLEWHITE CARVED MAHOGANY CARD TABLE

PLATE 10

27   HEPPLEWHITE INLAID MAHOGANY BONHEUR DU JOUR. *Cf* handles with those of 304.

PLATE 11

28 HEPPLEWHITE INLAID TULIPWOOD, THUJA AND HOLLY BONHEUR DU JOUR. With ormolu mounts, and long-favored
Late-Chippendale-Hepplewhite-Sheraton-Regency-Early-Victorian gallery. Courtesy of J. J. Wolff (Antiques) Ltd.,
New York City.

PLATE 12

29   HEPPLEWHITE INLAID MAHOGANY SERPENTINE-BOMBÉ COMMODE. With all original ormolu fittings. *Vide* 258; *Cf* side handles also of 376. Courtesy of Trevor, London.

30   HEPPLEWHITE JAPANNED AND DECORATED COMMODE. With identifying ormolu top edging, *sabots* and Parisian-type style capitals. Similar mounts appear on Dublin commodes formerly in Blaise Castle, Bristol, and in Newton Park, Bristol. Victoria & Albert Museum. Crown Copyright.

PLATE 13

31 HEPPLEWHITE CARVED MAHOGANY ARMCHAIR.
Cf rear feet of 32, 34 and 50.

32 HEPPLEWHITE CARVED BEECH ARMCHAIR

33 HEPPLEWHITE GILDED ARMCHAIR. The non-Germanic
origin could be determined only through the matching
ornamental details of a console (318) and its typical
Dublin-school painted decoration. Victoria & Albert
Museum. Crown Copyright.

34 HEPPLEWHITE CARVED AND GILDED ARMCHAIR

PLATE 14

35 HEPPLEWHITE CARVED MAHOGANY ARMCHAIR. *Cf* feet of 36-39.

36 HEPPLEWHITE CARVED BEECH ARMCHAIR

37 HEPPLEWHITE CARVED MAHOGANY ARMCHAIR

38 HEPPLEWHITE MAHOGANY ARMCHAIR

PLATE 15

39   HEPPLEWHITE PAINTED AND DECORATED BERGERE. Courtesy of Trevor, London.

PLATE 16

40   HEPPLEWHITE CARVED BEECH ARMCHAIR

41   HEPPLEWHITE CARVED BEECH ARMCHAIR.
Cf legs of 42 and 98.

42   HEPPLEWHITE CARVED BEECH SETTEE. Courtesy of J. J. Wolff (Antiques) Ltd., New York City.

PLATE 17

43 HEPPLEWHITE CARVED BEECH ARMCHAIR

44 HEPPLEWHITE CARVED BEECH ARMCHAIR.
From a Scottish collection.

45 HEPPLEWHITE CARVED BEECH ARMCHAIR

46 HEPPLEWHITE CARVED BEECH ARMCHAIR

PLATE 18

47 HEPPLEWHITE CARVED MAHOGANY ARMCHAIR

48 HEPPLEWHITE CARVED MAHOGANY ARMCHAIR

49 HEPPLEWHITE CARVED MAHOGANY ARMCHAIR

50 HEPPLEWHITE CARVED BEECH ARMCHAIR

PLATE 19

51 HEPPLEWHITE CARVED AND PAINTED SIDE CHAIR

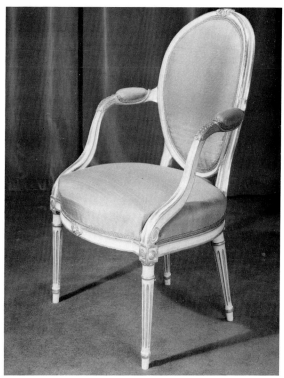

52 HEPPLEWHITE CARVED, PAINTED AND PARCEL-GILDED ELBOW CHAIR. *En suite* with 55. Courtesy of Trevor, London.

53 HEPPLEWHITE PAINTED ARMCHAIR IN NEEDLEPOINT. From the Countess of Kilmorey, Monroe Park, County Down. Courtesy of French & Co., New York City.

54 HEPPLEWHITE GILDED ARMCHAIR. From the Marquis of Salisbury, Hatfield House, Surrey.

PLATE 20

55 HEPPLEWHITE CARVED, PAINTED AND PARCEL-GILDED SETTEE. From a suite of 14 armchairs and 6 settees formerly contained in an old Irish residence. Courtesy of Trevor, London.

56 SHERATON CARVED, PAINTED AND DECORATED SETTEE

PLATE 21

57 HEPPLEWHITE CARVED MAHOGANY ARMCHAIR.
Matching 147 and 174. Victoria & Albert Museum.
Crown Copyright.

58 HEPPLEWHITE CARVED MAHOGANY ARMCHAIR

59 HEPPLEWHITE CARVED MAHOGANY ARMCHAIR

60 HEPPLEWHITE CARVED MAHOGANY SIDE CHAIR

PLATE 22

61 HEPPLEWHITE CARVED MAHOGANY ARMCHAIR.
Courtesy of Needham's Antiques, Inc., New York City.

62 HEPPLEWHITE CARVED MAHOGANY ARMCHAIR.
Courtesy of Needham's Antiques, Inc., New York City.

63 HEPPLEWHITE CARVED MAHOGANY SIDE CHAIR

64 HEPPLEWHITE CARVED MAHOGANY SIDE CHAIR

PLATE 23

65 HEPPLEWHITE CARVED MAHOGANY ARMCHAIR

66 HEPPLEWHITE CARVED MAHOGANY ARMCHAIR

67 HEPPLEWHITE CARVED MAHOGANY UPHOLSTERED SIDE CHAIR. *Vide* sideboard table, Pl VIII, *Dictionary of English Furniture.*

68 HEPPLEWHITE CARVED MAHOGANY ARMCHAIR. The legs reduced. Metropolitan Museum of Art, New York City.

PLATE 24

69 HEPPLEWHITE CARVED MAHOGANY ARMCHAIR. A typical Dublin model that has been authoritatively claimed as designed by Robert Adam. Metropolitan Museum of Art, New York City.

70 HEPPLEWHITE CARVED MAHOGANY SIDE CHAIR WITH HOLLY PANEL. Victoria & Albert Museum. Crown Copyright.

71 HEPPLEWHITE CARVED MAHOGANY SIDE CHAIR

72 HEPPLEWHITE CARVED MAHOGANY SIDE CHAIR

PLATE 25

73 HEPPLEWHITE CARVED AND INLAID MAHOGANY
ARMCHAIR. Victoria & Albert Museum. Crown
Copyright.

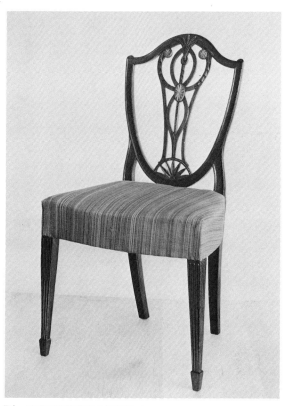

74 HEPPLEWHITE CARVED AND INLAID MAHOGANY
SIDE CHAIR. Victoria & Albert Museum. Crown
Copyright.

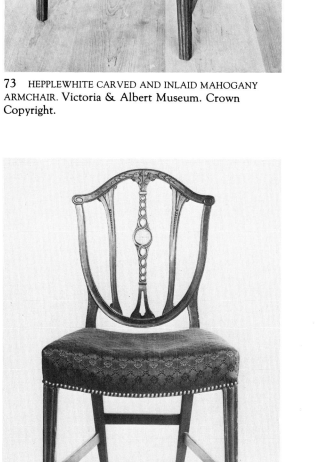

75 HEPPLEWHITE CARVED AND INLAID MAHOGANY
SIDE CHAIR. Philadelphia Museum of Art.

76 HEPPLEWHITE CARVED MAHOGANY ARMCHAIR

PLATE 26

77 HEPPLEWHITE MAHOGANY SIDE CHAIR CARVED WITH PRINCE-OF-WALES PLUMES. *Cf* front feet with 36-39.

78 HEPPLEWHITE CARVED MAHOGANY SIDE CHAIR. Victoria & Albert Museum. Crown Copyright.

79 HEPPLEWHITE CARVED MAHOGANY SIDE CHAIR

80 HEPPLEWHITE CARVED MAHOGANY ELBOW ARMCHAIR. *Vide* Percy Macquoid, *Age of Satinwood*, Fig. 179, an almost matching five-chair-back settee.

PLATE 27

81 HEPPLEWHITE CARVED MAHOGANY ARMCHAIR

82 HEPPLEWHITE CARVED MAHOGANY ARMCHAIR
WITH PRINCE-OF-WALES PLUMES

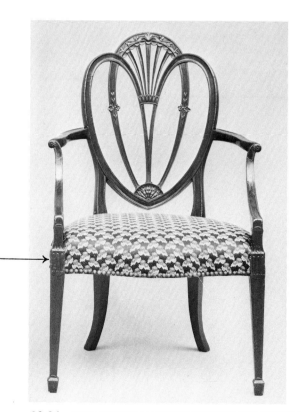

83-84 HEPPLEWHITE MAHOGANY HEART-AND-SHIELD BACK ARMCHAIRS CARVED WITH SHAMROCKS. A design
influencing the development of American seat furniture, including a set of chairs made for Governor Talbot of
Connecticut. *Cf* die of leg with 87. Metropolitan Museum of Art, New York City.

PLATE 28

85 HEPPLEWHITE MAHOGANY UPHOLSTERED
ARMCHAIR. *Cf* leg and foot of 231.

86 HEPPLEWHITE CARVED MAHOGANY UPHOLSTERED
TUB CHAIR

87 HEPPLEWHITE MAHOGANY UPHOLSTERED SETTEE. *Vide* matching dies of 83.

PLATE 29

88 HEPPLEWHITE CHAIRS AND SERVING TABLES IN THE DINING ROOM OF MOUNT JULIET, COUNTY KILKENNY. Courtesy
of the late Noel C. Hartnel, Dublin.

PLATE 30

89 HEPPLEWHITE CARVED MAHOGANY SIDE CHAIR

90 HEPPLEWHITE CARVED MAHOGANY SIDE CHAIR

91 HEPPLEWHITE CARVED MAHOGANY ELBOW CHAIR.
Vide Oliver Brackett, *English Furniture, Illustrated*, p. 236.
From Princess Elizabeth, Duchess of Edinburgh.

92 HEPPLEWHITE CARVED AND INLAID MAHOGANY
ARMCHAIR

PLATE 31

93 HEPPLEWHITE CARVED MAHOGANY UPHOLSTERED
ARMCHAIR. *En suite* with 176-177.

94 HEPPLEWHITE CARVED MAHOGANY SIDE CHAIR.
Cf 71-72.

95 HEPPLEWHITE CARVED AND INLAID MAHOGANY
ARMCHAIR. Featuring Prince-of-Wales plumes. *Cf* all
four feet with 47-48. Victoria & Albert Museum.
Crown Copyright.

96 HEPPLEWHITE CARVED AND INLAID MAHOGANY
ARMCHAIR. Victoria & Albert Museum. Crown
Copyright.

PLATE 32

97 HEPPLEWHITE CARVED MAHOGANY SLIPPER CHAIR WITH COMPASS SEAT. A design found in Pennsylvania and North German collections.

98 HEPPLEWHITE SHIELD-BACK ARMCHAIR IN NEEDLEPOINT. *Cf* legs of 41. Victoria & Albert Museum. Crown Copyright.

99 HEPPLEWHITE CANED SHIELD-BACK ARMCHAIR. *Cf.* 128. Victoria & Albert Museum. Crown Copyright.

100 HEPPLEWHITE CARVED AND INLAID MAHOGANY SIDE CHAIR

PLATE 33

101 HEPPLEWHITE CARVED AND GILDED PALMETTE-BACK ARMCHAIR

102 HEPPLEWHITE CARVED MAHOGANY PALMETTE-BACK ARMCHAIR

103 HEPPLEWHITE CARVED AND INLAID MAHOGANY ARMCHAIR

104 HEPPLEWHITE CARVED MAHOGANY BERGERE

PLATE 34

105   HEPPLEWHITE CARVED MAHOGANY SMALL UPHOLSTERED SETTEE

106   HEPPLEWHITE MAHOGANY UPHOLSTERED SETTEE

PLATE 35

107   HEPPLEWHITE PAINTED AND DECORATED ARMCHAIR

108   HEPPLEWHITE PAINTED AND DECORATED ARMCHAIR.
Metropolitan Museum of Art, New York City.

109   HEPPLEWHITE PAINTED AND DECORATED ARMCHAIR

110   HEPPLEWHITE PAINTED AND DECORATED HEART-
AND-SHIELD-BACK ARMCHAIR. Featuring Prince-of-Wales
plumes. From a private Scottish residence.

PLATE 36

111 SHERATON PAINTED AND DECORATED ARMCHAIR

112 SHERATON PAINTED AND DECORATED ARMCHAIR.
Courtesy of Needham's Antiques, Inc., New York City.

113 SHERATON PAINTED AND DECORATED CHAIR-BACK SETTEE. From Langford Court, Langford, Somerset.

PLATE 37

114 SHERATON PAINTED AND DECORATED ARMCHAIR.
Courtesy of Needham's Antiques, Inc., New York City.

115 SHERATON PAINTED AND DECORATED ARMCHAIR.
Victoria & Albert Museum. Crown Copyright.

116 SHERATON PAINTED AND DECORATED ARMCHAIR.
With figural medallion.

117 REGENCY CARVED, PAINTED AND DECORATED
ARMCHAIR. With figural medallion. *Cf* front legs of 94.
Victoria & Albert Museum. Crown Copyright.

PLATE 38

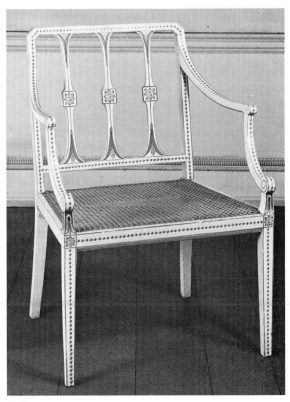

118 SHERATON PAINTED AND DECORATED ARMCHAIR

119 SHERATON PAINTED AND DECORATED ARMCHAIR. Victoria & Albert Museum. Crown Copyright.

120 SHERATON PAINTED AND DECORATED CANED SETTEE. Victoria & Albert Museum. Crown Copyright.

PLATE 39

121 SHERATON INLAID MAHOGANY ARMCHAIR. From a set of 2 arm, and 12 side chairs.

122 SHERATON SHELL-INLAID ELBOW CHAIR. The conch shell as in Dublin sideboard, Fig. 64, *Age of Satinwood.*

123 SHERATON CARVED AND INLAID WALNUT ARMCHAIR. From a set of twelve.

124 SHERATON CARVED MAHOGANY ARMCHAIR. Featuring Prince-of-Wales plumes. Formerly owned by Governor Edward Lloyd of Maryland.

PLATE 40

125 SHERATON CARVED MAHOGANY ARMCHAIR

126 SHERATON CARVED MAHOGANY ARMCHAIR.
Courtesy of Biggs of Maidenhead.

127 SHERATON CARVED MAHOGANY ARMCHAIR. A
matching side chair with compass seat, and plain rear
legs, is illustrated in the *Age of Satinwood*, Fig. 233.

128 SHERATON CARVED MAHOGANY SIDE CHAIR.
With compass seat. *Cf* front legs with 97 and 99.

PLATE 41

129   SHERATON CARVED MAHOGANY ARMCHAIR

130   SHERATON CARVED MAHOGANY ARMCHAIR

131   SHERATON INLAID AND DECORATED SATINWOOD
ARMCHAIR. Courtesy of Trevor, London.

132   REGENCY CARVED MAHOGANY SIDE CHAIR WITH
JAPANNED FIGURAL PANEL

PLATE 42

133   GEORGE III CARVED MAHOGANY ARMCHAIR

134   REGENCY MAHOGANY STRADDLE CHAIR

135   SHERATON CARVED MAHOGANY TUB CHAIR

136   SHERATON MAHOGANY TUB CHAIR

PLATE 43

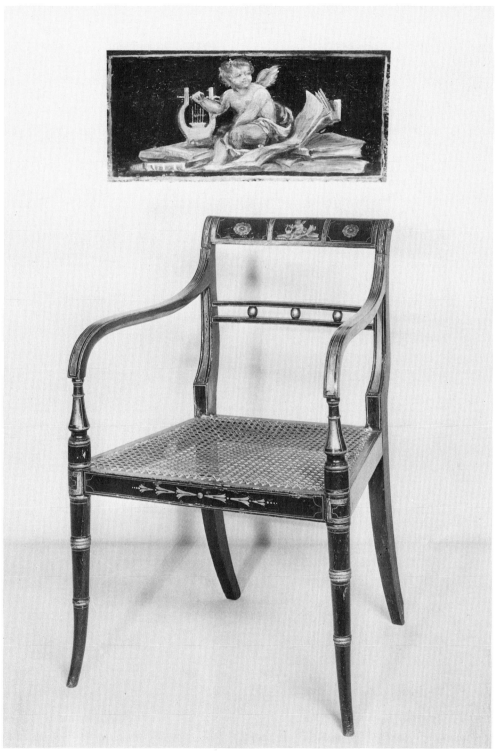

137   REGENCY DECORATED BLACK-AND-GOLD ARMCHAIR. With enlargement of its Cupid panel.

PLATE 44

138 REGENCY DECORATED BLACK-AND-GOLD
ARMCHAIR. Courtesy of Needham's Antiques, Inc.,
New York City.

139 REGENCY DECORATED BLACK-AND-GOLD
ARMCHAIR. Courtesy of Mallett & Son (Antiques)
Ltd., London, Geneva and New York.

140 REGENCY DECORATED BLACK-AND-GOLD
ARMCHAIR. Victoria & Albert Museum. Crown
Copyright.

141 REGENCY DECORATED BLACK-AND-GOLD SIDE CHAIR

PLATE 45

142 REGENCY CANED SIDE CHAIR. Victoria & Albert Museum. Crown Copyright.

143 REGENCY JAPANNED ARMCHAIR WITH ORMOLU MOUNTS. Victoria & Albert Museum. Crown Copyright.

144 REGENCY BRASS-INLAID MAHOGANY ARMCHAIR. Victoria & Albert Museum. Crown Copyright.

145 REGENCY ROSEWOOD-GRAINED AND BRASS INLAID SIDE CHAIR WITH ORMOLU MOUNTS

PLATE 46

146 LATE CHIPPENDALE
URN STAND

147 HEPPLEWHITE CARVED MAHOGANY URN STAND.
Matching 57 and 174.

148 HEPPLEWHITE CARVED
MAHOGANY URN STAND

PLATE 47

149 SHERATON INLAID SYCAMORE ENVELOPE TABLE

150 SHERATON INLAID MAHOGANY OCTAGONAL GAMING TABLE

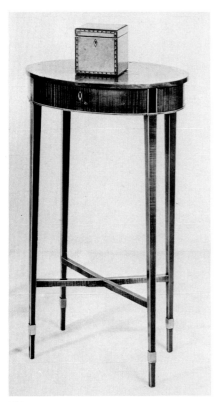

151 SHERATON INLAID SYCAMORE OCCASIONAL TABLE. **From an old Irish residence.**

152 REGENCY INLAID ROSEWOOD, MAHOGANY AND SATINWOOD OCCASIONAL TABLE

PLATE 48

153 HEPPLEWHITE CARVED AND INLAID ZEBRAWOOD PEMBROKE TABLE

154 HEPPLEWHITE INLAID SATINWOOD PEMBROKE TABLE

155 SHERATON PEMBROKE TABLE WITH DETERMINATIVE MARQUETRY FEATURES. *Cf* 346 and 369. Victoria & Albert Museum. Crown Copyright.

PLATE 49

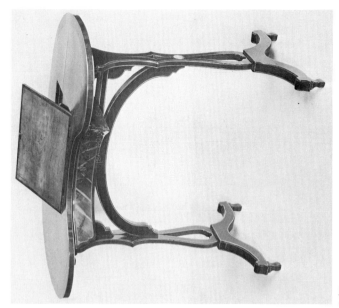

157 REGENCY INLAID MAHOGANY AND YEWWOOD KIDNEY-SHAPED WRITING TABLE

158 REGENCY MAHOGANY WHATNOT WITH ORMOLU MOUNTS. Courtesy of Trevor, London.

156 REGENCY INLAID ROSEWOOD WRITING TABLE. With lever lock.

PLATE 50

159   SHERATON INLAID MAHOGANY TAMBOUR WRITING
TABLE

160   SHERATON INLAID THUJA CYLINDER-FRONT
WRITING TABLE. Courtesy of Needham's Antiques, Inc.,
New York City.

PLATE 51

161 SHERATON INLAID BURL YEWWOOD CYLINDER-FRONT WRITING TABLE. Courtesy of Trevor, London.

162 SHERATON INLAID HOLLY AND AMARANTH BONHEUR DU JOUR. Courtesy of Trevor, London.

PLATE 52

163 REGENCY BRASS-INLAID ROSEWOOD AND ORMOLU BONHEUR DU JOUR

PLATE 53

164 REGENCY CARVED ROSEWOOD AND ORMOLU
BOOK CARRIER WITH TABLE STAND. Metropolitan
Museum of Art, New York City.

165 REGENCY CARVED ROSEWOOD AND ORMOLU
OPEN-SHELF STAND WITH BOOK SHELF. Courtesy of
Trevor, London.

PLATE 54

166 SHERATON BIRCH AND HOLLY MARQUETRY ARCHITECT'S TABLE

167 SHERATON INLAID BIRCH AND HOLLY CARLTON HOUSE WRITING TABLE

PLATE 55

168 SHERATON INLAID MAHOGANY CARLTON HOUSE WRITING TABLE. Courtesy of
J. J. Wolff (Antiques) Ltd., New York City.

169 REGENCY MAHOGANY LIBRARY TABLE WITH ORMOLU MOUNTS. With Dublin angular bail handles, and London
lever locks by Bramah. Cf 277-8.

PLATE 56

171   SHERATON INLAID SATINWOOD PEDESTAL DESK.
Courtesy of Trevor, London.

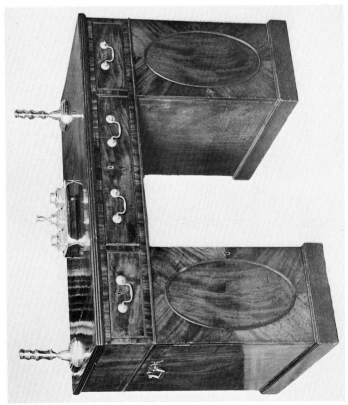

170   SHERATON MAHOGANY PEDESTAL DESK

PLATE 57

172   SHERATON INLAID MAHOGANY SERPENTINE PEDESTAL DESK. *Vide patera* of 178. Courtesy of Needham's Antiques, Inc., New York City.

PLATE 58

173   HEPPLEWHITE CARVED MAHOGANY CONCERTINA
CARD TABLE. *Vide* also R. W. Symonds, *Furniture
Making in 17th and 18th Century England*, Fig. 174, for
an even more readily identifiable Dublin example.

174   HEPPLEWHITE CARVED MAHOGANY CARD TABLE.
Matching 57 and 147.

PLATE 59

175   HEPPLEWHITE CARVED AND INLAID MAHOGANY CARD TABLE

176-177   HEPPLEWHITE CARVED MAHOGANY CARD TABLE AND STOOL

PLATE 60

178 SHERATON INLAID MAHOGANY CONSOLE. The patera, border and top edge bandings all important determinative treatments.

179 REGENCY INLAID MAHOGANY SIDE TABLE OR DESSERTE. With Egyptian terms. *Vide* 273 and 299.

180 REGENCY CARVED AND GILDED EAGLE CONSOLE. Courtesy of Jeremy, Ltd., London.

PLATE 61

181   REGENCY ORMOLU-MOUNTED ROSEWOOD SOFA TABLE. With highly characteristic handles, escutcheons, *sabots* and gallery treatment. A slightly later version is illustrated in R. W. Symonds, *Furniture-Making in 17th and 18th Century England*, Fig. 187.

182   REGENCY BRASS-INLAID AND ORMOLU-MOUNTED CALAMANDER SOFA TABLE. At Marlborough House. Reproduced by gracious permission of Her Majesty, the late Queen Mary.

PLATE 62

183   REGENCY INLAID ROSEWOOD SOFA WRITING
TABLE

184   REGENCY INLAID AND DECORATED SMALL CENTRE
TABLE. *Cf sabots* with 181. Courtesy of Trevor,
London.

185   REGENCY BRASS-INLAID ROSEWOOD SOFA TABLE WITH ORMOLU MOUNTS. Courtesy of Trevor, London.

PLATE 63

186   SHERATON INLAID MAHOGANY SOFA TABLE

187   REGENCY SOFA TABLE WITH INKWORK DECORATION

PLATE 64

188 REGENCY BRASS-INLAID AMBOINA AND ROSEWOOD SOFA TABLE. One of three recorded as made in 1816 for Princess Charlotte. At Buckingham Palace. Reproduced by gracious permission of Her Majesty, the late Queen Mary. Copyright *Country Life*.

189 REGENCY BRASS-INLAID ROSEWOOD SOFA TABLE. *Cf* support of 195. Victoria & Albert Museum. Crown Copyright.

PLATE 65

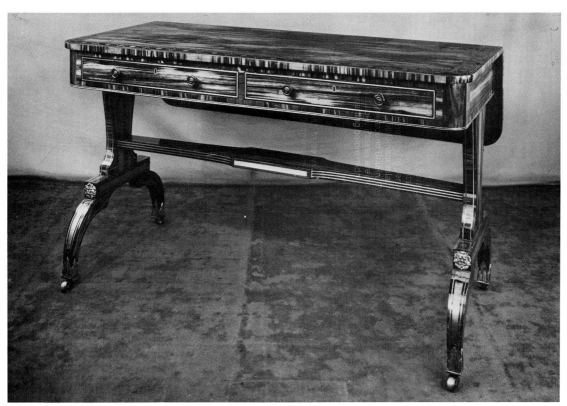

190   REGENCY INLAID CALAMANDER SOFA TABLE

191   REGENCY INLAID ROSEWOOD SOFA TABLE WITH ORMOLU MOUNTS. Courtesy of Trevor, London.

PLATE 66

194   REGENCY BRASS-INLAID ROSEWOOD CARD TABLE

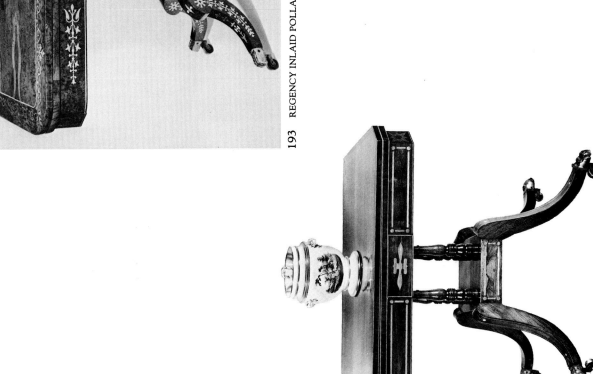

193   REGENCY INLAID POLLARD OAK CARD TABLE

192   REGENCY INLAID ROSEWOOD CARD TABLE. *Cf* dot-dash inlay with 299.

PLATE 67

197 REGENCY INLAID ROSEWOOD CARD TABLE WITH ORMOLU MOUNTS. Routinely described as English.

196 REGENCY CARVED MAHOGANY CARD TABLE. Described as a New York example, possibly by Duncan Phyfe.

195 REGENCY INLAID CARD TABLE. One of a pair described as "the finest New England examples known."

PLATE 68

198 LATE GEORGIAN MAHOGANY TRIPOD TABLE WITH ENVELOPE TOP

199 LATE GEORGIAN CARVED MAHOGANY PIECRUST TABLE

200 SHERATON INLAID SATINWOOD DROP-LEAF TRIPOD TABLE. **Matching 219.**

201 SHERATON INLAID AND SPIRALLY-TURNED OCTAGONAL TRIPOD TABLE

PLATE 69

204 LATE GEORGIAN MAHOGANY DUMBWAITER

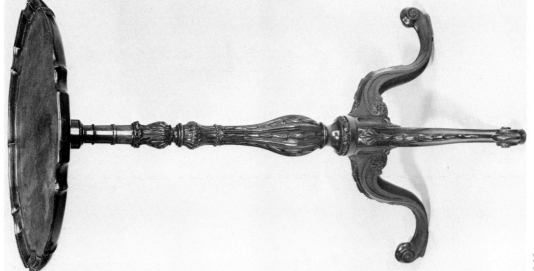

202 HEPPLEWHITE CARVED MAHOGANY PIECRUST
TABLE

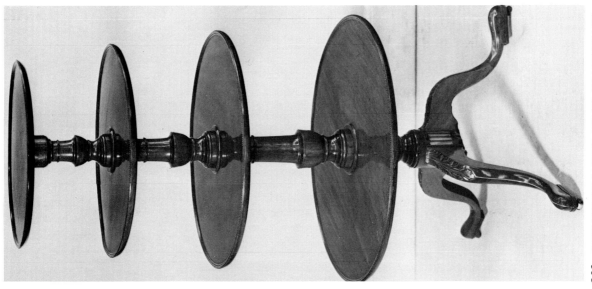

203 HEPPLEWHITE CARVED AND INLAID MAHOGANY
FOUR-TIER DUMBWAITER. Courtesy of J. J. Wolff
(Antiques) Ltd., New York City.

PLATE 70

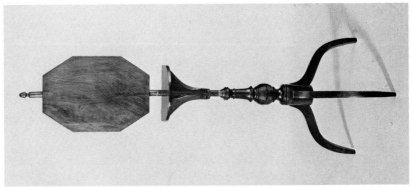

207 REGENCY MAHOGANY TRIPOD CANDLE STAND WITH SCREEN

205 GEORGE III MAHOGANY MODEL DUMBWAITER

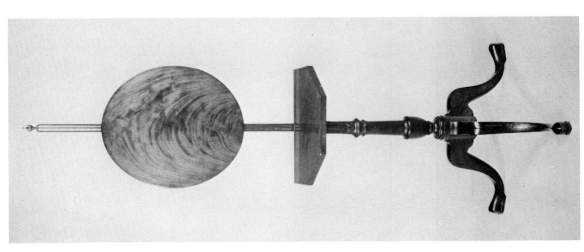

206 GEORGE III MAHOGANY TRIPOD CANDLE STAND WITH SCREEN

PLATE 71

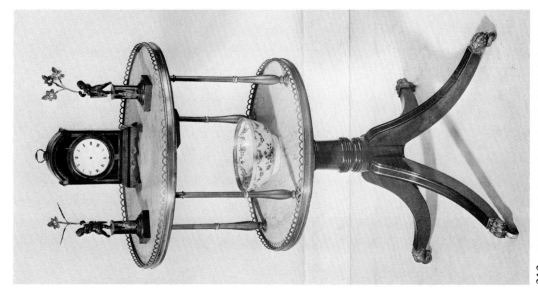

210 REGENCY BRASS-INLAID MAHOGANY, ORMOLU
AND MARBLE TWO-TIER DUMBWAITER

209 REGENCY MAHOGANY TRIPOD BOOKSTAND

208 REGENCY MAHOGANY DUMBWAITER WITH
ORMOLU GALLERIES

PLATE 72

211 REGENCY MAHOGANY TWO-TIER TRIPOD STAND
WITH SPINDLE GALLERY

212 REGENCY MAHOGANY TRIPOD BOOKSTAND WITH
ORMOLU MOUNTS

PLATE 73

213 SHERATON SATINWOOD MARQUETRY SMALL
DRUM TABLE. With revolving top.

214 SHERATON INLAID MAHOGANY DRUM TABLE

PLATE 74

215   REGENCY INLAID ROSEWOOD SMALL DRUM TABLE

216   REGENCY INLAID MAHOGANY DRUM TABLE

PLATE 75

217   REGENCY PARCEL-GILDED ZEBRAWOOD LIBRARY
TABLE. From Ralph Dutton, Hinton Ampner House.
Copyright *Country Life*.

218   REGENCY PARCEL-GILDED MAHOGANY DRUM
TABLE

PLATE 76

219   SHERATON INLAID SATINWOOD BREAKFAST TABLE.
Matching 200.

220   SHERATON INLAID MAHOGANY BREAKFAST TABLE

PLATE 77

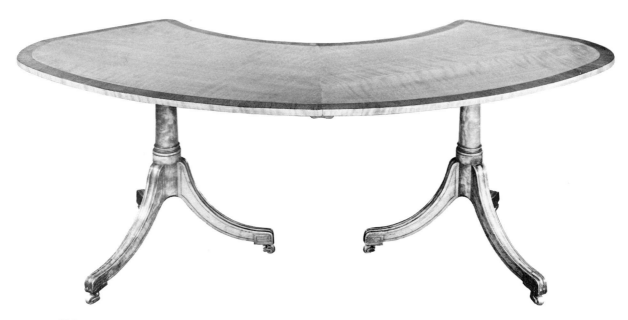

221   SHERATON INLAID SATINWOOD AND ROSEWOOD TWO-PEDESTAL HUNT TABLE. Courtesy of Biggs of
Maidenhead.

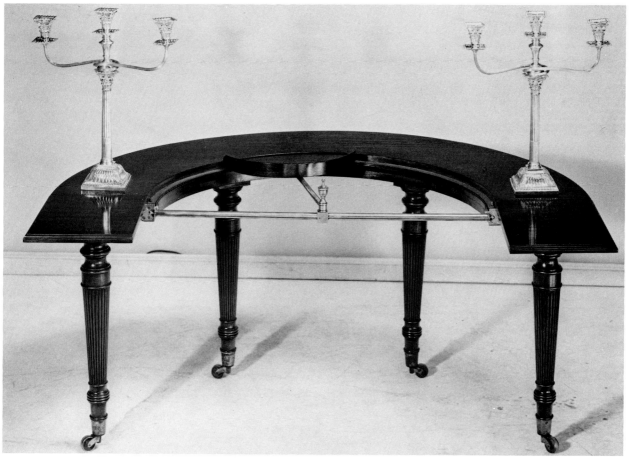

222   REGENCY MAHOGANY AND ORMOLU HEARTHSIDE DRINKING TABLE

PLATE 78

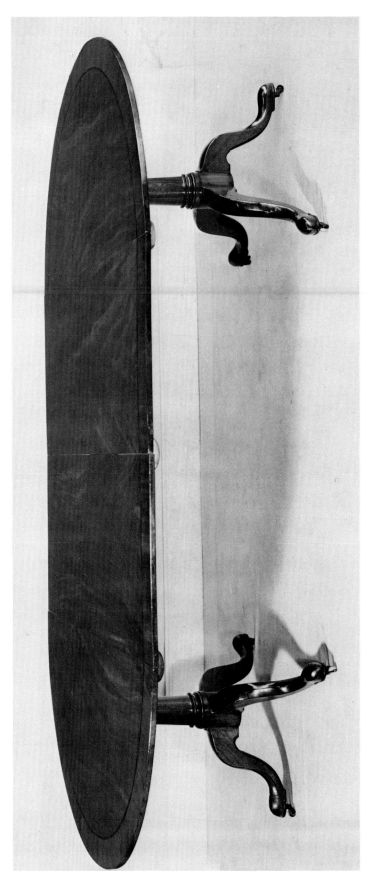

223   GEORGE III INLAID MAHOGANY TWO-PEDESTAL DINING TABLE

PLATE 79

224   SHERATON PADAUK THREE-PEDESTAL DINING TABLE

PLATE 80

225   SHERATON INLAID MAHOGANY TWO-PEDESTAL DINING TABLE

114

PLATE 81

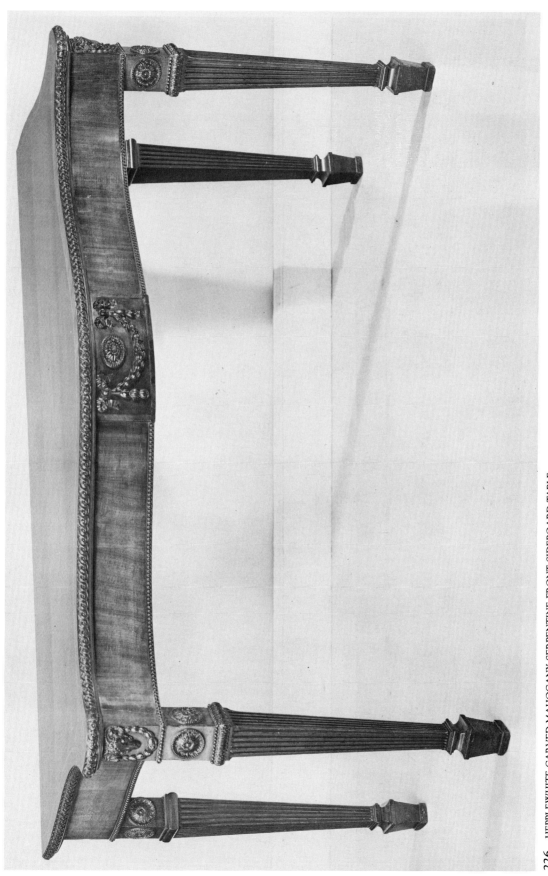

226   HEPPLEWHITE CARVED MAHOGANY SERPENTINE-FRONT SIDEBOARD TABLE

PLATE 82

227 HEPPLEWHITE CARVED MAHOGANY SIDEBOARD TABLE. Courtesy of Charles Lumb & Sons Ltd., Harrogate.

PLATE 83

228 GEORGE III CARVED MAHOGANY AND ORMOLU SIDEBOARD TABLE, PEDESTALS AND URNS. In the dining room at Mount Juliet, County Kilkenny. Courtesy of the late Noel C. Hartnell, Dublin.

PLATE 84

229   PAIR GEORGE III CARVED MAHOGANY PEDESTALS AND URNS

PLATE 85

230 HEPPLEWHITE CARVED AND INLAID MAHOGANY DINING TABLE. The top featuring a distinctive checkered border. Victoria & Albert Museum. Crown Copyright.

PLATE 86

231 HEPPLEWHITE MAHOGANY SERPENTINE-FRONT SIDEBOARD TABLE. A similar Regency wine cooler is illustrated in Jourdain & Rose, *English Furniture: the Georgian Period*, p. 163, as "Mid-eighteenth century."

PLATE 87

232   VIEW OF THE DINING ROOM IN MOUNT JULIET, COUNTY KILKENNY. Courtesy of the late Noel C. Hartnell, Dublin.

PLATE 88

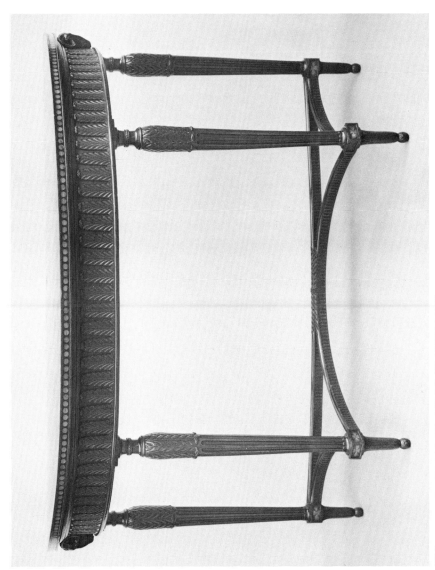

234 HEPPLEWHITE CARVED AND INLAID MAHOGANY SIDEBOARD TABLE. *En suite* Metropolitan Museum of Art, New York City.

233 HEPPLEWHITE CARVED AND INLAID MAHOGANY PEDESTAL AND URN. The inlaid work by William Moore. *Cf* also Fig. 6-7 Tea trays, *Dictionary of English Furniture.* Courtesy of French & Co., Inc., New York City.

PLATE 89

236   REGENCY ROSEWOOD SERVING TABLE WITH ORMOLU MOUNTS AND GALLERY. Courtesy of Trevor, London.

235   REGENCY CARVED MAHOGANY SIDEBOARD TABLE

PLATE 90

237   HEPPLEWHITE INLAID MAHOGANY SIDEBOARD

238   HEPPLEWHITE INLAID MAHOGANY SIDEBOARD. *Vide* also Jourdain & Rose, *English Furniture: the Georgian Period.* 154.

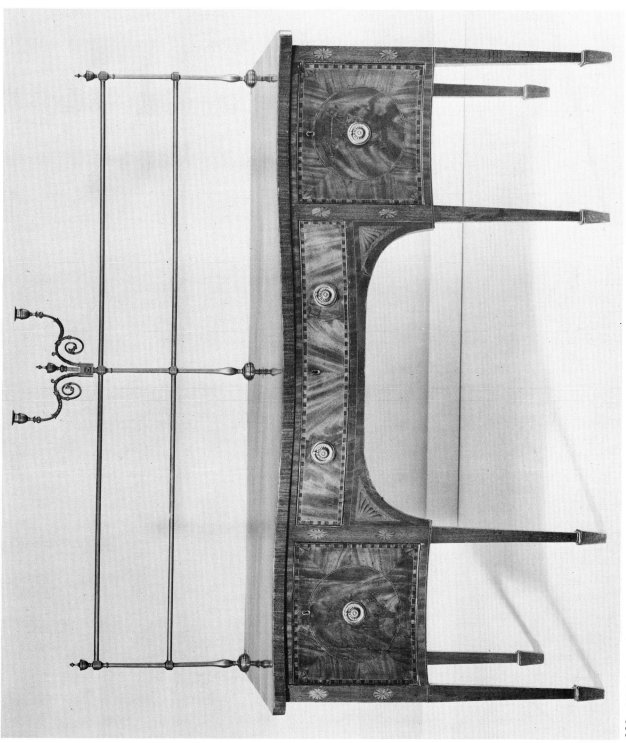

239   SHERATON INLAID MAHOGANY SIDEBOARD WITH ORMOLU GALLERY

PLATE 92

240 SHERATON CARVED AND INLAID MAHOGANY SIDEBOARD

241 SHERATON INLAID MAHOGANY SIDEBOARD

PLATE 93

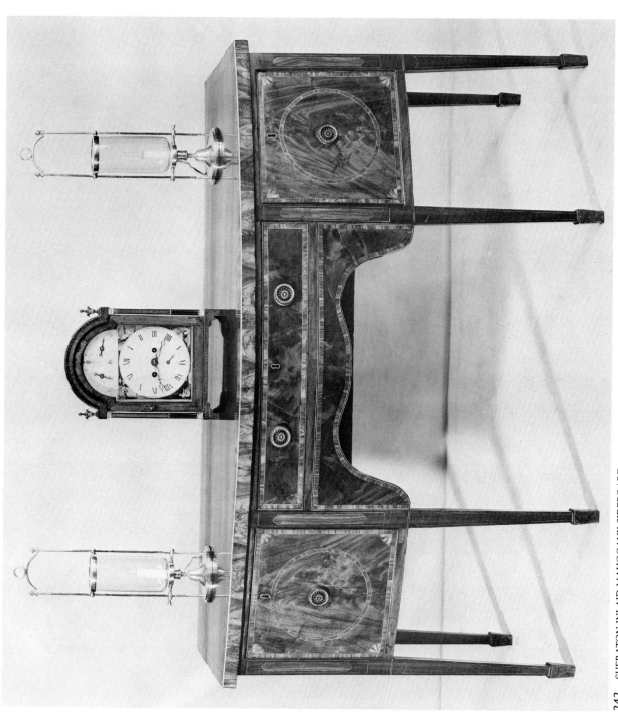

242 SHERATON INLAID MAHOGANY SIDEBOARD

PLATE 94

243 REGENCY INLAID MAHOGANY SIDEBOARD

PLATE 95

244   REGENCY INLAID MAHOGANY PEDESTAL SIDEBOARD. With favorite Dublin pattern handles as in 162, 252 and 356.

PLATE 96

245 REGENCY BRASS-INLAID ROSEWOOD PEDESTAL SIDEBOARD. Victoria & Albert Museum. Crown Copyright.

PLATE 97

246 GEORGE III INLAID MAHOGANY SERPENTINE-FRONT COMMODE. *Cf* banding of 257. Courtesy of J. J. Wolff (Antiques) Ltd., New York City.

247 HEPPLEWHITE INLAID SYCAMORE SERPENTINE-FRONT COMMODE. **Handles replaced.**

PLATE 98

248 HEPPLEWHITE INLAID MAHOGANY SERPENTINE-FRONT COMMODE.
With original handles. *Cf* Valanced base of 298.

249 HEPPLEWHITE INLAID MAHOGANY SERPENTINE-FRONT COMMODE. With handles
of a distinctive Dublin pattern.

PLATE 99

250   SHERATON INLAID MAHOGANY BOW-FRONT COMMODE

251   SHERATON INLAID MAHOGANY BOW-FRONT COMMODE

PLATE 100

252 SHERATON INLAID MAHOGANY BOW-FRONT COMMODE.
With handles of a distinctive Dublin pattern, as in 162, 244 and 356.

253 REGENCY INLAID MAHOGANY SEMI-ELLIPTICAL COMMODE.
With original handles. Courtesy of J. J. Wolff (Antiques) Ltd.,
New York City.

PLATE 101

254 HEPPLEWHITE LABURNUM MARQUETRY SERPENTINE-BOMBE COMMODE. The striped markings somewhat similar to those of another Dublin-favored veneer. *Vide 255.*

255 HEPPLEWHITE INLAID YEW SERPENTINE-FRONT COMMODE

PLATE 102

256   HEPPLEWHITE MAHOGANY SERPENTINE-FRONT COMMODE

257   HEPPLEWHITE MAHOGANY SERPENTINE-FRONT COMMODE. Inlaid with a distinctive checkered link-chain banding. The handles are of a Dublin Chippendale-Hepplewhite pattern. Victoria & Albert Museum. Crown Copyright.

PLATE 103

258   HEPPLEWHITE INLAID MAHOGANY SERPENTINE-BOMBÉ COMMODE. With all original handles, and escutcheons. Courtesy of Trevor, London.

259   HEPPLEWHITE INLAID MAHOGANY SERPENTINE-BOMBÉ COMMODE. (Handles changed.)

PLATE 104

260 HEPPLEWHITE INLAID MAHOGANY SMALL COMMODE

261 SHERATON INLAID MAHOGANY SMALL 'COMMODE'

262 SHERATON INLAID MAHOGANY AND SATINWOOD SMALL 'COMMODE'.
Courtesy of Trevor, London.

263 REGENCY INLAID SATINWOOD SMALL 'COMMODE' WITH GRILLE PANELS

PLATE 105

264   SHERATON INLAID AND DECORATED SATINWOOD COMMODE. With silver-plated handles.

265   REGENCY INLAID SATINWOOD COMMODE

PLATE 106

266   REGENCY INLAID MAHOGANY LOW OPEN-SHELF CABINET.
Courtesy of Jeremy, Ltd., London.

267   REGENCY INLAID ROSEWOOD MARBLE-TOP CABINET WITH GRILLE PANELS

PLATE 107

268   REGENCY INLAID ROSEWOOD LOW CABINET WITH GRILLE PANELS.
Cf the Parisian-Directoire foot here with 269, 272, 274, 281, 283.

269   REGENCY INLAID ROSEWOOD LOW CABINET WITH GRILLE PANELS

PLATE 108

270 REGENCY INLAID ROSEWOOD AND WALNUT OYSTERWOOD MARQUETRY
COMMODE WITH WATERCOLOR PANELS

271 REGENCY BRASS-INLAID ROSEWOOD LOW OPEN-SHELF CABINET. With ormolu grilles and paw feet.

PLATE 109

272 REGENCY LOW CABINET WITH BLACK-AND-GOLD JAPANNED DECORATION

273 REGENCY LOW CABINET WITH INKWORK DECORATION. Egyptian terms also appear in 299.
Victoria & Albert Museum. Crown Copyright.

PLATE 110

274   REGENCY LOW CABINET WITH BLACK-AND-GOLD DECORATION

275   REGENCY LOW CABINET WITH INKWORK DECORATION.
Courtesy of Trevor, London.

PLATE 111

277 REGENCY INLAID SATINWOOD SECRETARY CABINET. *Cf* handles of 169, 278.
Courtesy of J. J. Wolff (Antiques) Ltd., New York City.

276 SHERATON INLAID AND DECORATED SATINWOOD SECRETARY CABINET

PLATE 112

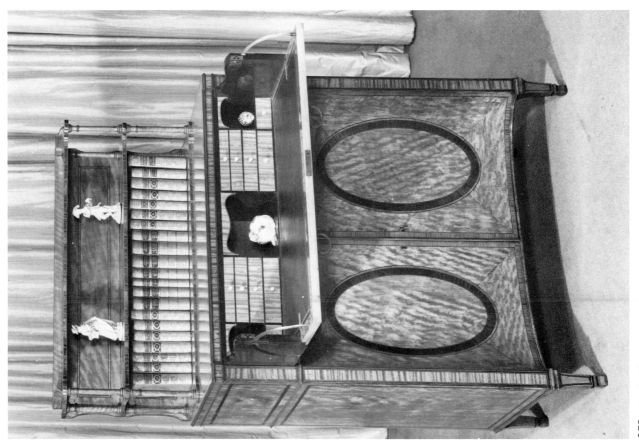

279 SHERATON INLAID SATINWOOD SECRETAIRE WITH OPEN SHELVES.
Courtesy of Trevor, London.

278 SHERATON INLAID SATINWOOD CYLINDER-FRONT SECRETAIRE WITH
OPEN SHELVES. Courtesy of Needham's Antiques, Inc., New York City.

PLATE 113

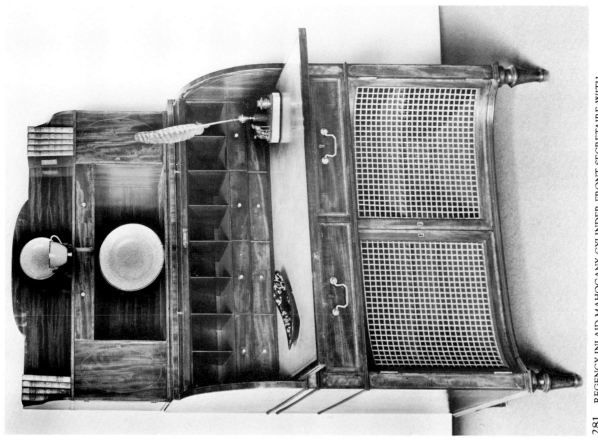

281   REGENCY INLAID MAHOGANY CYLINDER-FRONT SECRETAIRE WITH OPEN SHELVES. Courtesy of Needham's Antiques, Inc., New York City.

280   SHERATON INLAID MAHOGANY SECRETAIRE WITH OPEN SHELVES. Courtesy of Needham's Antiques, Inc., New York City.

PLATE 114

283 REGENCY INLAID MAHOGANY OPEN-SHELF CABINET. *Vide also Age of Satinwood*, Fig. 201.

282 REGENCY INLAID MAHOGANY OPEN-SHELF CABINET

PLATE 115

285 REGENCY BRASS-INLAID AND ORMOLU MOUNTED MAHOGANY OPEN-
SHELF CABINET

284 REGENCY INLAID MAHOGANY AND ORMOLU OPEN-SHELF CABINET.
Courtesy of Needham's Antiques, Inc., New York City.

PLATE 116

286   SHERATON INLAID MAHOGANY BREAKFRONT CABINET. Courtesy of Trevor, London.

PLATE 117

287   SHERATON INLAID MAHOGANY SECRETARY CABINET

PLATE 118

288   REGENCY INLAID CYLINDER-FRONT WRITING CABINET. Courtesy of Trevor, London.

PLATE 119

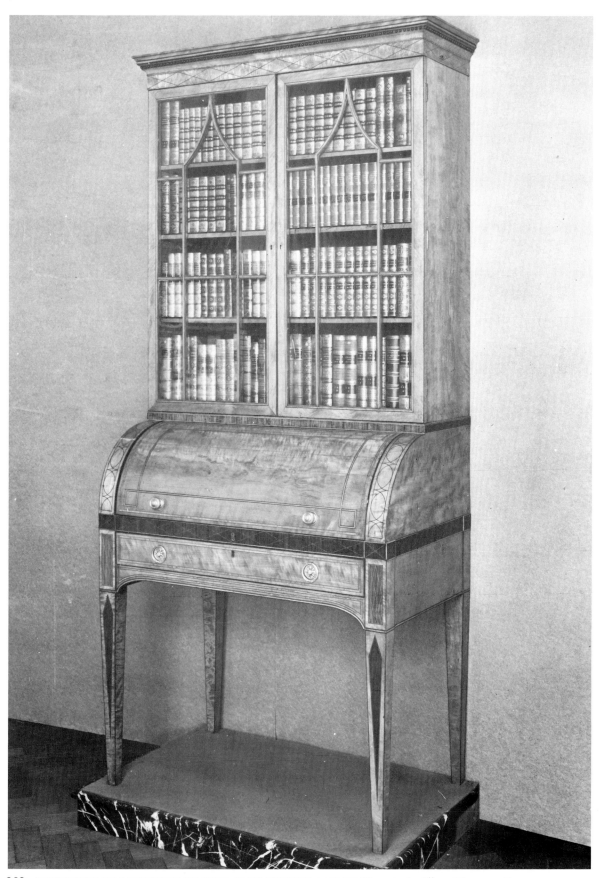

289   REGENCY INLAID SATINWOOD CYLINDER-FRONT WRITING CABINET. Victoria & Albert Museum. Crown
Copyright.

PLATE 120

290   GEORGE III CARVED AND INLAID MAHOGANY CHEST-ON-CHEST. With original handles and inset ivory key plates; the base a Late Chippendale interpretation.

PLATE 121

291   HEPPLEWHITE INLAID MAHOGANY WARDROBE.

PLATE 122

292   HEPPLEWHITE MAHOGANY BOOK OR CHINA CABINET

PLATE 123

293   HEPPLEWHITE INLAID SATINWOOD SECRETAIRE. With scrolled and fret-pierced pediment, the interior small drawers featuring holly panels. Courtesy of Trevor, London.

PLATE 124

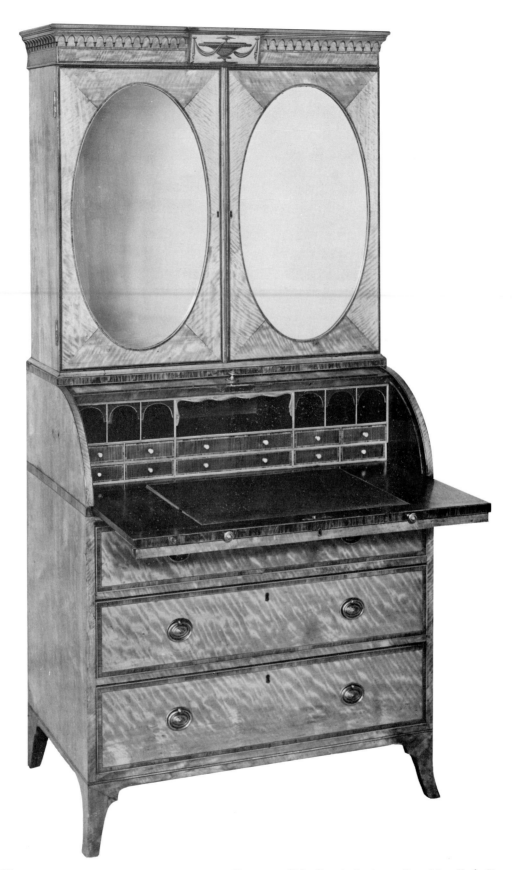

294   HEPPLEWHITE INLAID AVODIRE SECRETARY. Courtesy of Needham's Antiques, Inc., New York City.

PLATE 125

295 SHERATON INLAID MAHOGANY CYLINDER-FRONT SECRETARY. With original ormolu handles and finials.
Courtesy of Trevor, London.

PLATE 126

296   SHERATON INLAID MAHOGANY SECRETAIRE. With favorite conch-shell inlay.

PLATE 127

297   REGENCY INLAID SATINWOOD SECRETAIRE. With favorite conch-shell inlay.
Original handles and finials.

PLATE 128

298   REGENCY INLAID WEST INDIAN SATINWOOD AND SABICU CLOCK CABINET. *Vide* p. 24, 30.

PLATE 129

299 REGENCY INLAID ZEBRAWOOD SECRETAIRE WITH EGYPTIAN TERMS. *Cf* 273. As a Dublin innovation, the writing drawer sides are cut back and feature the most superior, recessed pivot hinges and quadrant stays. Victoria & Albert Museum. Crown Copyright.

PLATE 130

300　GEORGE III MAHOGANY BREAKFRONT BOOKCASE WITH CLEFT PEDIMENT

PLATE 131

301   GEORGE III MAHOGANY ARCHITECTURAL BREAKFRONT BOOKCASE. The mock-fluted cornice inlaid with
Sheraton fan paterae. From an old Georgian residence on the Isle of Wight.

PLATE 132

302   GEORGE III INLAID MAHOGANY BREAKFRONT BOOKCASE WITH SCROLLED PEDIMENT. The cupboard doors with
full width book-matched veneers, original handles as more generally found on earlier Dublin cabinetwork.

PLATE 133

303   HEPPLEWHITE MAHOGANY BREAKFRONT BOOKCASE.

PLATE 134

304   SHERATON INLAID MAHOGANY SECRETARY-BOOKCASE. Original handles. From Lord Hatfield, Hatfield House, Surrey.

PLATE 135

305 GEORGE III CARVED MAHOGANY BREAKFRONT BOOKCASE WITH SCROLLED PEDIMENT

PLATE 136

306   HEPPLEWHITE INLAID MAHOGANY BREAKFRONT BOOKCASE WITH MARQUETRY PANELS

PLATE 137

307   HEPPLEWHITE SYCAMORE MARQUETRY PEMBROKE TABLE

308   HEPPLEWHITE INLAID MAHOGANY CARD TABLE. Courtesy of Trevor, London.

PLATE 138

309   HEPPLEWHITE INLAID MAHOGANY DRESSING TABLE WITH MARQUETRY PANELS. Victoria & Albert Museum.
Crown Copyright.

PLATE 139

310   HEPPLEWHITE SYCAMORE MARQUETRY CONSOLE TABLE

PLATE 140

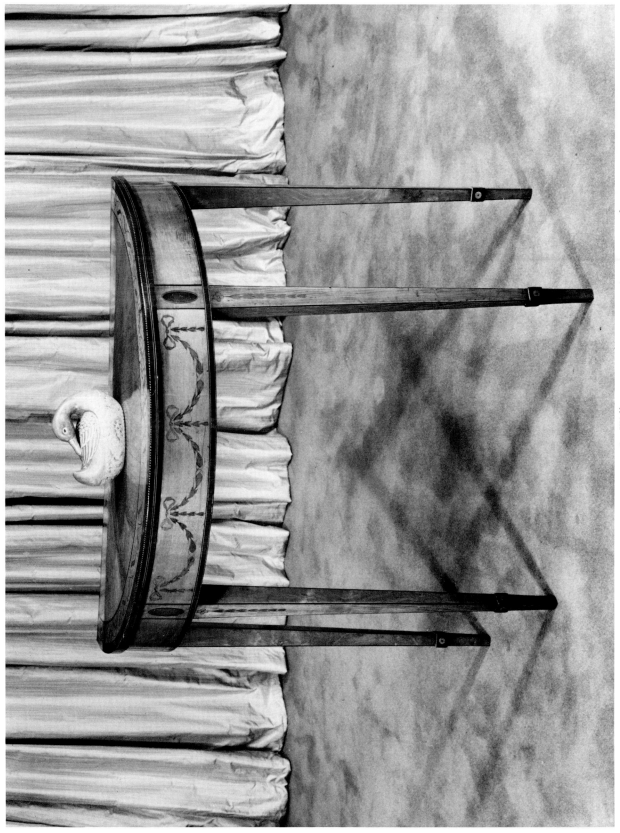

311   HEPPLEWHITE SATINWOOD AND HOLLY MARQUETRY CONSOLE TABLE. By William Moore. Courtesy of Trevor, London.

PLATE 141

312   HEPPLEWHITE SATINWOOD MARQUETRY CONSOLE TABLE. By William Moore. Courtesy of Trevor, London.

PLATE 142

313   SHERATON INLAID MAHOGANY PEMBROKE TABLE. Inlaid by William Moore. *Cf* 339. From the J. P. Morgan Collection, New York City.

PLATE 143

314   SHERATON INLAID SATINWOOD SIDE TABLE MOUNTED IN ORMOLU. By William Moore.

PLATE 144

315   SHERATON INLAID SATINWOOD AND HOLLY SIDE TABLE. By William Moore.

PLATE 145

316 SHERATON MARQUETRY SIDE TABLE WITH SPHINX PANEL. Inlaid by William Moore. Courtesy of French & Co., Inc., New York City.

PLATE 146

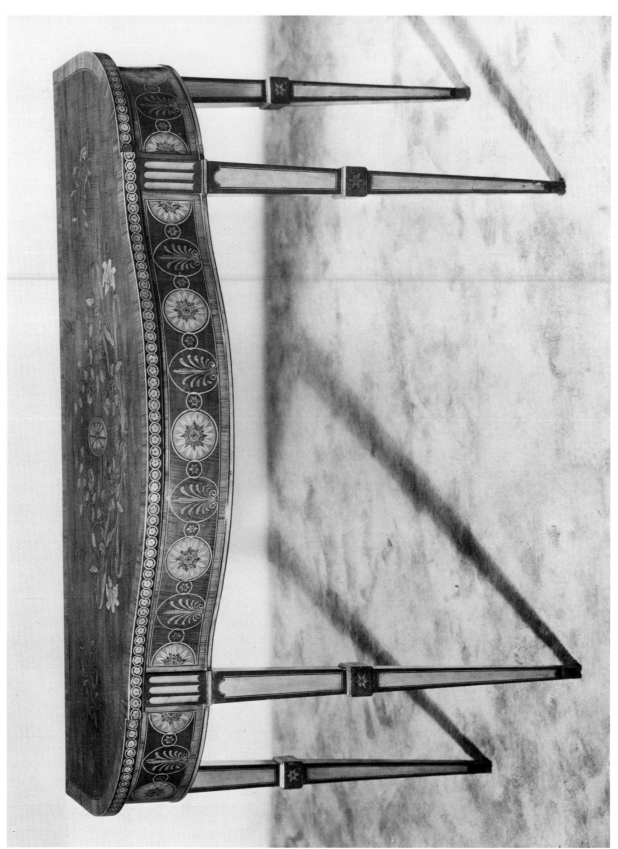

317   SHERATON MARQUETRY SIDE TABLE. By William Moore.

PLATE 147

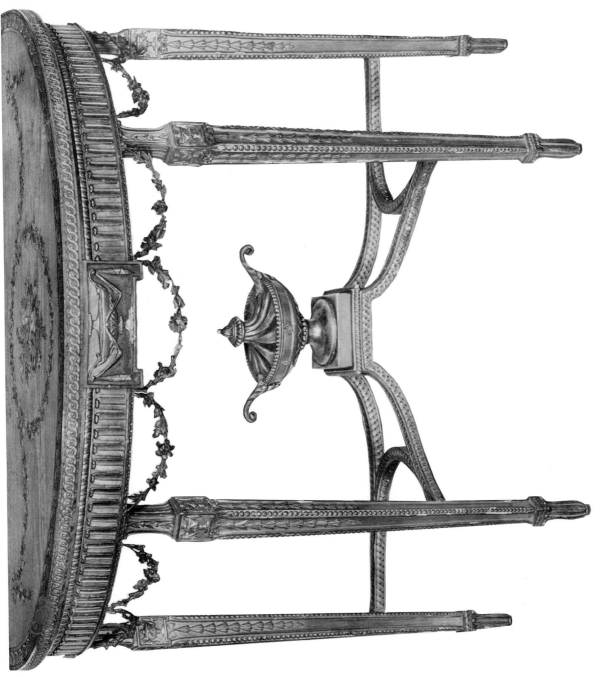

318. HEPPLEWHITE GILDED CONSOLE TABLE. The top painted with festooning encircling a bouquet. *En suite with* 33.

PLATE 148

319 SHERATON GILDED CONSOLE TABLE WITH INLAID AND DECORATED TOP. Courtesy of Trevor, London.

PLATE 149

320 SHERATON GILDED CONSOLE WITH INLAID MARBLE TOP. Courtesy of Asprey & Company Ltd., London.

PLATE 150

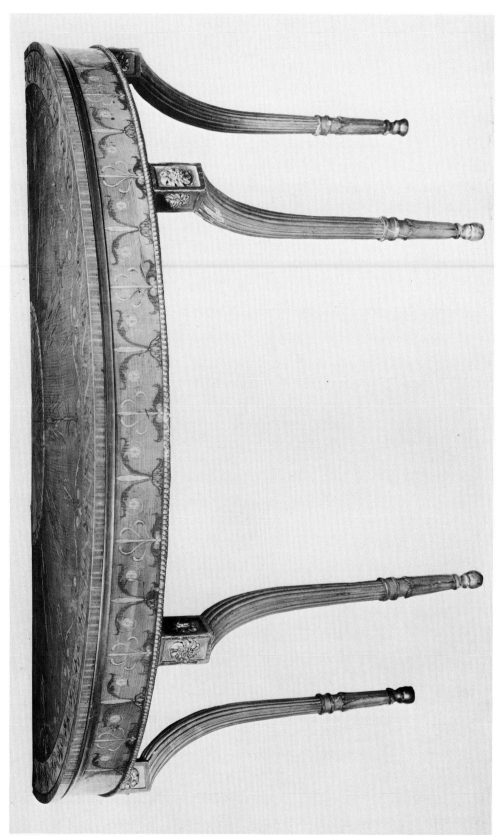

321   SHERATON SYCAMORE MARQUETRY AND GILDED CONSOLE

PLATE 151

322 SHERATON PAINTED, DECORATED AND PARCEL-GILDED SIDE TABLE

PLATE 152

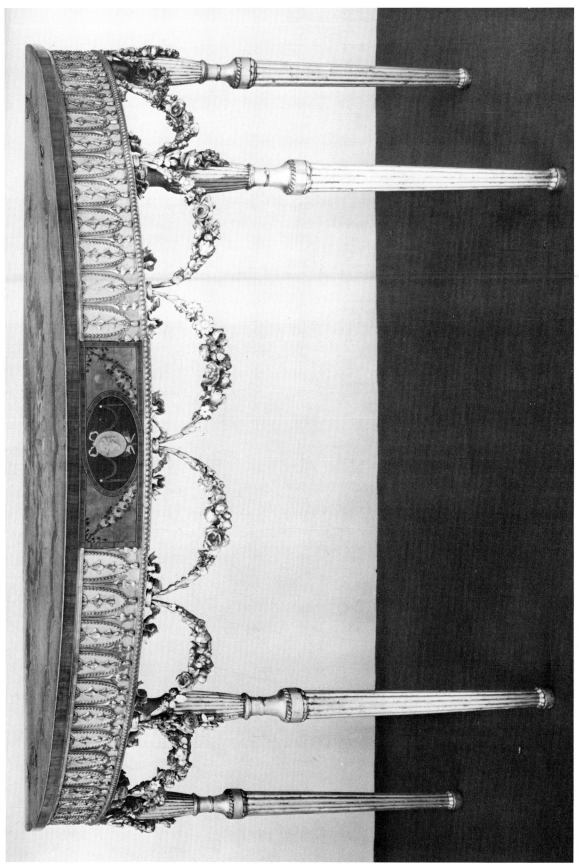

323 SHERATON INLAID, DECORATED AND GILDED SIDE TABLE. *Vide also Age of Satinwood* 212-213, and *Dictionary of English Furniture*, III, p. 273, Fig. 60. Victoria & Albert photograph, courtesy of The Lady Lever Art Gallery.

PLATE 153

324 SHERATON PAINTED, DECORATED AND GILDED CONSOLE TABLE. The decorations executed on copper. Victoria & Albert Museum. Crown Copyright.

PLATE 154

325 HEPPLEWHITE MARQUETRY SERPENTINE-BOMBÉ COMMODE MOUNTED IN ORMOLU. Circa 1765. The same mascaron apron mount appears on other Dublin examples falsely assigned to Langlois; one recently obtained a record auction price of $232,000; *vide Antiques World* (February 1980). *Vide* p. 21. Victoria & Albert Museum. Crown Copyright.

PLATE 155

326 HEPPLEWHITE MARQUETRY SERPENTINE-BOMBÉ COMMODE MOUNTED IN ORMOLU. Circa 1770. The marquetry more characteristic even than the patterns and high quality of the supposedly English metalwork. Victoria & Albert Museum. Crown Copyright.

PLATE 156

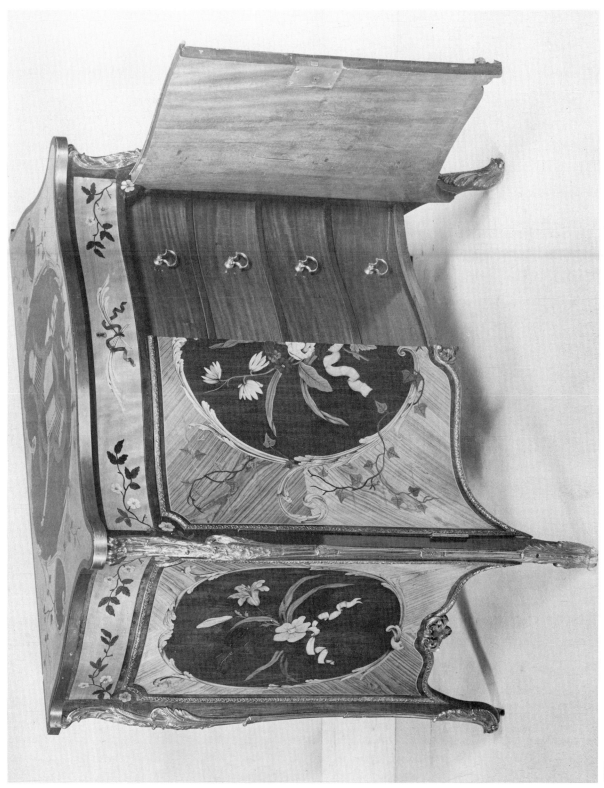

327   HEPPLEWHITE OLIVEWOOD AND HOLLY MARQUETRY COMMODE MOUNTED IN ORMOLU. Companion to the following. From Castle Moyle, County Kerry.

PLATE 157

328   HEPPLEWHITE OLIVEWOOD AND HOLLY MARQUETRY COMMODE MOUNTED IN ORMOLU. The same fine stile and apron mounts and top edging appear in Jourdain & Rose, *English Furniture: the Georgian Period*, p. 113, dated "Mid-eighteenth century"; the stile mounts in the *Dictionary of English Furniture*, vol. 1, 141. From Castle Moyle, County Kerry.

PLATE 158

329   HEPPLEWHITE SATINWOOD MARQUETRY SERPENTINE-FRONT COMMODE. Victoria & Albert Museum. Crown Copyright.

PLATE 159

330   HEPPLEWHITE MARQUETRY SERPENTINE COMMODE

PLATE 160

331 HEPPLEWHITE MARQUETRY BREAKFRONT COMMODE WITH ORMOLU MOUNTS. From the Earl of Shaftesbury, St. Giles House, Dorset. Courtesy of Christie, Manson & Woods, London.

PLATE 161

332 HEPPLEWHITE ORMOLU-MOUNTED COMMODE WITH CHINESE DECORATED LACQUER PANELS. A plainer exampl is illustrated in the *Dictionary of English Furniture*, Fig. 10. From Ragley Hall, Warwick. Courtesy of Christie, Manson & Woods, London.

PLATE 162

333 HEPPLEWHITE INLAID SABICU SERPENTINE-FRONT COMMODE. Courtesy of Mallett & Son (Antiques) Ltd., London, Geneva and New York.

PLATE 163

334   HEPPLEWHITE SYCAMORE MARQUETRY SERPENTINE COMMODE

PLATE 164

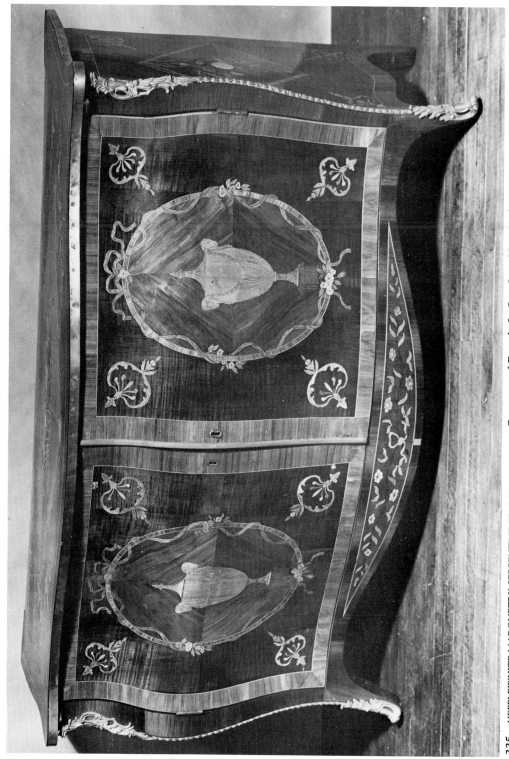

335 HEPPLEWHITE MARQUETRY SERPENTINE-FRONT COMMODE. Courtesy of French & Co., Inc., New York City.

PLATE 165

336   HEPPLEWHITE SYCAMORE PARQUETRY AND MARQUETRY COMMODE. Courtesy of Trevor, London.

PLATE 166

337 HEPPLEWHITE SYCAMORE AND SATINWOOD MARQUETRY COMMODE.
By William Moore. Courtesy of J. J. Wolff (Antiques) Ltd., New York City.

338 HEPPLEWHITE SYCAMORE AND SATINWOOD MARQUETRY COMMODE. By William Moore.
Courtesy of Christie, Manson & Woods, Ltd., London.

PLATE 167

339   HEPPLEWHITE SATINWOOD MARQUETRY COMMODE. Inlaid William Moore. *Cf* 313.
Philadelphia Museum of Art.

PLATE 168

340   SHERATON SATINWOOD MARQUETRY COMMODE. By William Moore.

PLATE 169

341 SHERATON INLAID MAHOGANY COMMODE. By William Moore. Courtesy of Mallet & Son (Antiques) Ltd., London, Geneva and New York.

PLATE 170

342   SHERATON INLAID SATINWOOD COMMODE. By William Moore.

204

PLATE 171

343 SHERATON INLAID SYCAMORE COMMODE. By William Moore. Courtesy of Jeremy Ltd., London.

PLATE 172

344 SHERATON SATINWOOD MARQUETRY COMMODE. By William Moore. A matching tambour writing table has been published as designed by Robert Adam (*Connoisseur*, December, 1919, p. 214).

PLATE 173

345 SHERATON INLAID SATINWOOD AND HOLLY COMMODE. *Vide* also *Age of Satinwood*, 159.

346 SHERATON INLAID AND DECORATED SATINWOOD COMMODE.
Vide also *Age of Satinwood*, Fig. 160. Philadelphia Museum of Art.

PLATE 174

347   SHERATON INLAID AND DECORATED SYCAMORE COMMODE. Lady Lever Collection, Port Sunlight, Cheshire.

PLATE 175

348 SHERATON SYCAMORE MARQUETRY ARMORIAL
COMMODE. With arms of Wright impaling Carrington.
Original handles.

349 REGENCY MARQUETRY COMMODE WITH ORMOLU MOUNTS

PLATE 176

352 SHERATON INLAID SATINWOOD TRIPOD TABLE. A similar example was acquired by Queen Mary for Buckingham Palace. *Vide* H. Clifford Smith, *Buckingham Palace*, 280. Courtesy of Trevor, London.

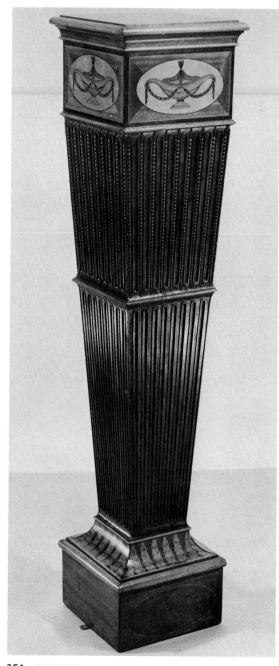

350 SHERATON INLAID MAHOGANY AND HOLLY KNIFE URN. With over a dozen key bandings and borders. Victoria & Albert Museum. Crown Copyright.

351 SHERATON INLAID MAHOGANY AND HOLLY TERM. Courtesy of J. J. Wolff (Antiques) Ltd., New York City.

PLATE 177

353   SHERATON PAINTED, DECORATED AND PARCEL
GILDED CORNER 'COMMODE.' Photograph courtesy of
the Philadelphia Museum of Art.

354   SHERATON PAINTED AND DECORATED 'COMMODE'

PLATE 178

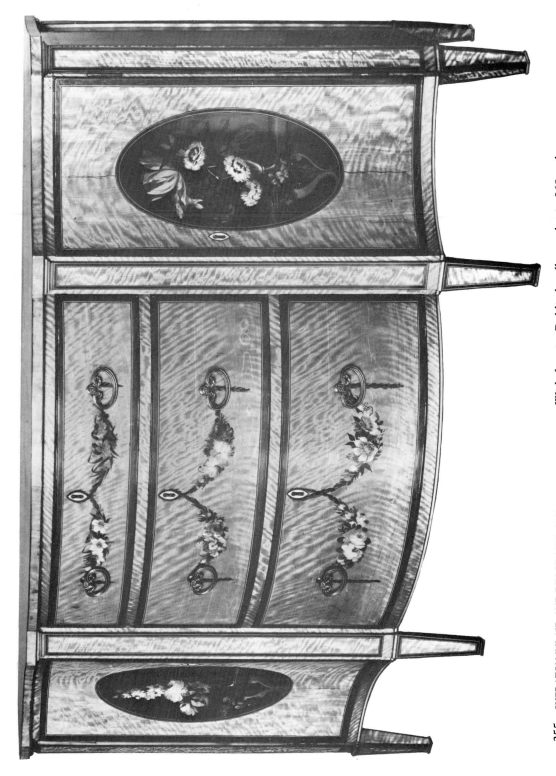

355 SHERATON INLAID AND DECORATED SATINWOOD COMMODE. With favorite Dublin handles as also in 368 and 372. Victoria & Albert Museum. Crown Copyright.

PLATE 179

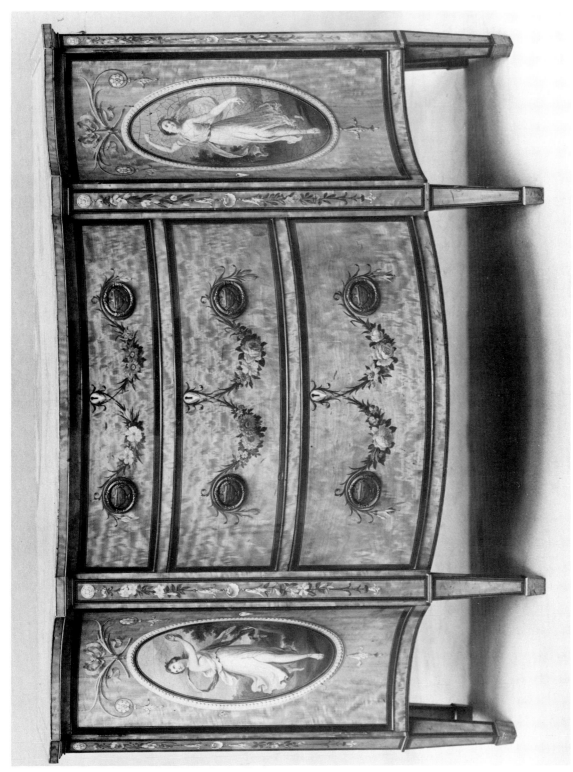

356 SHERATON INLAID AND DECORATED SATINWOOD COMMODE. With favorite Dublin handles as also in 162, 244 and 252. Victoria & Albert Museum. Crown Copyright.

PLATE 180

357   REGENCY INLAID AND DECORATED SATINWOOD COMMODE. With grille panels. *Cf* keyhole festooning with 355 and 356. From an old Irish residence. Courtesy of Trevor, London.

PLATE 181

358   HEPPLEWHITE SYCAMORE MARQUETRY BONHEUR DU JOUR. *Cf* 361. Courtesy of J. J. Wolff (Antiques) Ltd.,
New York City.

PLATE 182

359   SHERATON SYCAMORE MARQUETRY CYLINDER-FRONT BONHEUR DU JOUR

PLATE 183

360   HEPPLEWHITE SYCAMORE MARQUETRY CABINET ON TABLE STAND. *Vide* detail: 361. Victoria & Albert Museum. Crown Copyright.

PLATE 184

361   DETAIL OF CABINET, 360, SHOWING CHARACTERISTIC DUBLIN MARQUETRY OF CURVING STEMS OF ROSE
BLOSSOMS AND LEAVES

PLATE 185

362   HEPPLEWHITE AMARANTH AND HAREWOOD MARQUETRY FALL-FRONT SECRETAIRE WITH OPEN SHELVES. Original *sabots* as in 335 and 364. Courtesy of Asprey & Company Ltd., London.

PLATE 186

363 HEPPLEWHITE MARQUETRY AND PARQUETRY SERPENTINE-BOMBÉ CABINET. Supposedly the work of Thomas Chippendale. Typical Dublin ormolu stile mounts, *sabots* and top edging. From the Earl of Tankerville, Chillingham Castle, Northumberland.

PLATE 187

364 HEPPLEWHITE MARQUETRY CABINET MOUNTED IN ORMOLU. The diced light-and-dark bandings of exactly the same make up as those surrounding the marquetry and parquetry panels of 363. Courtesy of Christie, Manson and Woods, Ltd., London.

PLATE 188

365   HEPPLEWHITE INLAID HAREWOOD SECRETARY-CABINET. With applied astragals. Courtesy of Asprey &
Company Ltd., London.

PLATE 189

366 SHERATON INLAID AND DECORATED SATINWOOD CABINET WITH GRILLE PANELS

PLATE 190

367   SHERATON INLAID AND DECORATED SATINWOOD CYLINDER-FRONT SECRETAIRE. Courtesy of Biggs of Maidenhead.

PLATE 191

368   SHERATON INLAID AND DECORATED SATINWOOD CABINET WITH GILDED FINIALS. Favorite Dublin handles as in 355 and 372. From the family of Sir Richard Arkwright. Courtesy of Biggs of Maidenhead.

PLATE 192

369 SHERATON SATINWOOD MARQUETRY SECRETARY-BOOKCASE. Victoria & Albert
Museum. Crown Copyright.

PLATE 193

370 HEPPLEWHITE INLAID SATINWOOD BREAKFRONT CABINET. With Moore type inlays. From the Earl of Carnovan.

PLATE 194

371   SHERATON INLAID MAHOGANY SECRETARY-CABINET. With lateral wire-mesh panels.

PLATE 195

372   SHERATON CARVED, INLAID AND DECORATED SATINWOOD BUREAU-CABINET. Presented by Admiral Nelson to Lady Hamilton in Naples, *circa* 1800. The same handles appear in Pl 178 and 191. Courtesy of the National Gallery of Victoria, Melbourne.

PLATE 196

373 REGENCY INLAID AND DECORATED MAHOGANY AND SATINWOOD SECRETAIRE

PLATE 197

374   REGENCY INLAID AND DECORATED SATINWOOD SECRETARY-CABINET WITH MIRROR PANELS

PLATE 198

375   REGENCY INLAID SATINWOOD DINING-ROOM CABINET.

PLATE 199

376   LATE CHIPPENDALE MAHOGANY DOUBLE CHEST-OF-DRAWERS. With original Regency long-bearded lion-mask
bail handles. Courtesy of Needham's Antiques, Inc., New York City.

PLATE 200

377-378   TWO OF A SET OF TEN MURAL PANELS PAINTED IN OIL BY ANGELICA KAUFFMANN, IN 1772, FOR RATHFARNHAM CASTLE, NEAR DUBLIN. Recorded in the Georgian Society (of Ireland) Records, 1913. Brought to New York City in 1916 by Karl Freund.

PLATE 201

379 PROVINCIAL MAHOGANY CHEST-OF-DRAWERS. With orignially applied maker's label of "John Pettit, Waterford, 1813."

Index

[Italic figures refer to illustrations]